CORVETTE
1968–1982

Mike Mueller

MBI Publishing Company

First published in 2000 by MBI Publishing
Company, 729 Prospect Avenue, PO Box 1,
Osceola, WI 54020-0001 USA

The information in this book is true and complete
to the best of our knowledge. All recommendations
are made without any guarantee on the part of the
author or Publisher, who also disclaim any liability
incurred in connection with the use of this data or
specific details.

We recognize that some words, model names
and designations, for example, mentioned herein
are the property of the trademark holder. We use
them for identification purposes only. This is not an
official publication.

MBI Publishing Company books are also available
at discounts in bulk quantity for industrial or sales-
promotional use. For details write to Special Sales
Manager at Motorbooks International Wholesalers
& Distributors, 729 Prospect Avenue, PO Box 1,
Osceola, WI 54020-0001 USA.

Library of Congress Cataloging-in-Publication Data
Mueller, Mike.
     Corvette, 1968-1982 / Mike Mueller.
       p. cm.— (Sports car color history)
     Includes index.
     ISBN 0-7603-0418-1 (pbk. : alk. paper)
     1. Corvette automobile. I. Title. II. Series.
TL215.C6 M839724 2000
629.222'2—dc21   99-086043

On the front cover: The Corvette's third
generation run offered a little bit of everything to
sports car buyers. The LT-1 Stingray, introduced
in 1970, ranked as one of the breed's best all-
around performers. The Collector's Edition,
offered in 1982, featured more pizzazz than
Corvette customers had ever seen to that point.
Phil Vitale, of Port St. Lucie, Florida, owns the
1970 LT-1 coupe shown on this cover. The 1982
Collectors Edition is owned by Dan Holton of
Gainesville, Florida.

On the frontispiece: This little decal served as a
warning to all stoplight challengers in 1970 that
they were about to be eaten alive by Chevy's
meanest mouse motor, the 370-horsepower LT-1
350 small-block.

On the title page: Shrinking demand influenced
Chevrolet officials to let the sun go down on the
Corvette after 1975. A droptop model wouldn't
return until 1986. This Bright Yellow 1975
Stingray roadster is owned by Bill Tower of Plant
City, Florida.

On the back cover: The 1972 Stingray was the
last Corvette to feature traditional chrome
bumpers front and rear. A dent-resistant plastic
nose was added in 1973, followed by a bump-
proof plastic tail in 1974. Dennis Hold, of
Punta Gorda, Florida, owns the Mille Miglia
Red 1972 coupe shown here. The sliver 1975
convertible is owned by Bob Bateman of Port
Charlotte, Florida.

Edited by Paul Johnson
Designed by Dan Perry

Printed in China

Contents

Acknowledgments

I can't let any of you read any further into this epic without introducing you to the many people who went above and beyond the call of duty to help me miss yet another deadline. First, I have to do the obligatory family kudo thing, beginning with my sister, Kathy Young, and her husband, Master Sergeant Frank Young of the Illinois State Police. Kathy and Frank once made the mistake of insinuating that their fabulous home in Savoy, Illinois, was mine too. Can't take it back now. Same goes for Ma and Pa—Jim Sr. and Nancy Mueller—in Champaign, Illinois. Don't know what I would do without a free place to stay during my many photo junkets through the Midwest.

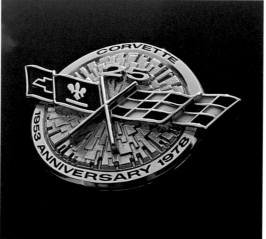

My brother-in-law, Officer Frank, has also proven especially helpful during photo shoots, as have my brothers Dave Mueller of Thomasboro, Illinois, and Jim Mueller Jr. of Champaign. Don't worry, guys, the check's in the mail, as always.

Worth more than all of that free labor combined is my wife, Joyce, who truly does know how to put the mule in Mueller. Her contributions to my projects can't be listed here, nor would she want some of them to be. Suffice it to say that I am one of the luckiest men on the face of the earth, if not the luckiest.

And speaking of incredibly good-looking young women, I would like to offer thanks to the "Comets," my 10-and-under Sandy Plains League girls softball team. While they didn't help me meet this deadline, they did make the struggle much more enjoyable. Chelsea Tucker, Michelle Gergel, Wesleigh Coskey, Savannah and Sierra McGrath, Carly Migdall, Courtney Nicklas, Kendall Reed, Kristi Lemieux, Caitie Cirou, Bridget Monroe, Colleen Evans, Lauren Smith, Casey Baker—you go, girls!

Back to business . . .

Various people responded to my pleas for supportive artwork for this book. Photographer Tom Glatch once again sent a couple of fabulous color frames down from Wisconsin. Archival black-and-white images came from author Pete Licastro, legendary Corvette historian Noland Adams, Charlie Brown at the St. Louis Mercantile Library, longtime friend and auto writer Bob Ackerson, and automotive literature collector/dealer Walter Miller. Two former bosses of mine, Donald Farr at Petersen Publishing in Florida and *Automobile Quarterly* editor Jonathan Stein, graciously helped me locate literally tons of valuable historical photography—too bad I couldn't use it all here. And I'll never be able to repay Chuck Schifsky, senior editor at *Motor Trend*, for coming to my aid as if I was an old friend in need. Such kindness must be catchy out west. *Motor Trend's* editor-in-chief, C. Van Tune, has also never failed to pick up the phone with a friendly hello whenever I've called for help or advice. Former *Motor Trend* (and *Hot Rod*) editor Eric Dahlquist's patience and kind cooperation over the last few years ranks as priceless as well.

Gary and Eric Mortimer of the National Corvette Restorers Society saved my bacon more than once too. Any Corvette fan couldn't lose by joining the NCRS—call them in Cincinnati at (513) 385-8526. NCRS judge and 1970–72 Corvette expert Terry MacManmon in Berwyn, Illinois, was especially helpful when it came time to write about the stillborn LS-7 454 V-8. Like all NCRS guys, Terry knows his stuff.

So do Bill Tower (Plant City, Florida) and Ray Quinlan (Champaign, Illinois), two veteran Corvette enthusiasts who have always been there to help keep me from stumbling too much. GM Powertrain man Jack Underwood too has often made it his job to take me in and raise. Thanks to Jack, I was able to spend more than one moment on the phone with veteran GM engineering legends Tom Langdon and Gib Hufstader, who both were there in 1969 when Duntov was promoting Corvette horsepower like it was going out of style. Too bad it was.

Finally, I have to make mention of Mike Yager and Steve Wiedman at Mid America Designs, Inc. Not only have Mike and Steve always welcomed me into their fabulous shop and museum, located among the cornfields outside Effingham, Illinois, they also invited me to serve as a VIP (their designation, not mine) judge for their 25th anniversary Corvette Funfest, held September 18–19, 1999. There, I had the pleasure of spending about three hours listening to former chief engineer Dave McLellan spin a yarn or two. Like Zora always did, Dave seems to have cornered the market in patience. What a gentleman and scholar.

Last, but certainly not least, I can't close without offering my gratitude to all the men and women who took the time to roll out their Corvettes for my Hasselblad. In general order of appearance, they are 1972 LT-1 coupe (blue), Larry Tritt, Woodstock, Georgia; 1977 coupe (red), Bill Nollenberger, Alpharetta, Georgia; 1967 Sting Ray, Bob Wolter, Champaign, Illinois; 1982 Collectors Edition, Dan Holton, Gainesville, Florida; 1996 Collectors Edition, Jim Morris, Winter Haven, Florida; 1969 ZL-1, Roger and Dave Judski, Roger's Corvette Center, Maitland, Florida; 1968 L-89 427 coupe (blue), Elmer and Dean Puckett, Elgin, Illinois; 1968 427 coupe (silver), Guy Landis, Kutztown, Pennsylvania; 1970 coupe (yellow), Phil Vitale, Port St. Lucie, Florida; 1971 454 convertible (blue), Tom Biltcliff, Topton, Pennsylvania; 1972 coupe (dark red), Dennis Hold, Punta Gorda, Florida; 1967 L-88, Bill Tower, Plant City, Florida; 1968 L-88 coupe, Lou Groebner, Corvette City, Highland Park, Illinois; 1971 LS-6 coupe, Jim MacDougald, Port Richey, Florida; 1970 LS-6 Chevelle SS 454, Dr. Sam TreBeck, Knoxville, Illinois; 1970 LT-1 convertible, Phil Vitale, Port St. Lucie, Florida; 1972 LT-1 coupe, Steve and Nora Gussack, Winter Springs, Florida; 1970–1/2 Camaro Z/28, Kevin Emberton, Edmonton, Kentucky; 1975 convertible (yellow), Bill Tower, Plant City, Florida; 1973 coupe (yellow) and 1974 454 coupe (blue), Robert Boynton Jr., Palm Harbor, Florida; 1975 convertible (silver), Bob Bateman, Port Charlotte, Florida; 1976 coupe (orange), Paul and Nancy Pearson, Lakeland, Florida; 1978 Indy Pace Car replica, Bill Tower, Plant City, Florida; 1979 L-82 coupe (black), Jerry Miller, Zephyrhills, Florida; 1981 two-tone coupe, Mike and Sharon Kelly, Portage, Indiana; and 1984 coupe serial number 00001, Dick Gonyer, Bowling Green, Ohio.

A hearty thanks and best wishes go to you all.

—Mike Mueller

AMERICA'S SPORTS CAR PURSUES PERFECTION

Preparations for one of the biggest birthday parties Detroit has ever seen are underway even as you read this, and the anniversary date itself is still some three years away. Forget all that ridiculous Y2K paranoia. The real headlines will be made in 2003 when Chevrolet's fantastic plastic two-seater will mark its 50th year on the automotive scene.

A half-century old? The Corvette? A half-century young would be more like it. All those years, all the trials and tribulations, and the Corvette looks none the worse for wear. That no other American car (Ford's F-series pickup truck celebrated its 50th in 1998, Cadillac's DeVille doesn't really count and Eldorado's many different faces rules it out on a technicality) can claim anything close to this longevity record is one thing. Zora Arkus-Duntov's dream machine is not only an unprecedented survivor, it also stands out as one of the few pleasures of life that actually has gotten better with age. Make that much better.

If only Corvette drivers could say the same. But then they wouldn't need cars like this to lead them to the nearest fountain of youth. From its humble beginnings in 1953, the Corvette has never failed in its role as a time machine capable of restoring its middle-aged owner's slackening sex appeal, at least in his mind. To hell with reality. Once behind a Corvette's wheel, any man becomes irresistible to women of all ages, preferably half his. That's a supernatural fact.

Back in the real world, the plain truth is that the Corvette also has never failed to excite all kinds of drivers, male or female, young or old, as this country's supreme performance machine. They don't call it "America's only sports car" for nothing. With absolutely no apologies whatsoever to the Dodge boys, the Corvette deserves this exclusive honor for various reasons, not the least of which is its established track record. Come back in 50 years, Viper fans, and we'll see what you've got.

Fifty years and five generations of Corvettes—one can only wonder if Harley Earl himself could have envisioned such a lengthy legacy when he first began the push for his little six-cylinder showcar in the early 1950s. While no one today dares doubt the Corvette's reason to be, there are, however, some who do feel the numbers don't quite add up. One, two, three, four, five—five generations? In many opinions, the figure should read six: 1953–55, 1956–62, 1963–67, 1968–82, 1984–96, and 1997–present. According to these kibitzers, even though the 1953–62 group all rolled on the same basic solid-axle chassis, the many upgrades made in 1956 should have established a break between the Corvette's first three pioneering models and the much improved solid-axles that followed. *Road & Track* apparently agreed in its March 1983 issue, which trumpeted the arrival of the "new 5th-generation Corvette."

According to General Motors' finger- and toe-counters, the fifth-generation Corvette arrived in January 1997. It was Chevrolet officials who cast the Corvette bloodline in stone by letting it slip a few years back that the next great model would be coded "C5"—the 5, of course, for five generations. Clearly Chevy people didn't

The third-generation Corvette began life with chrome bumpers at both ends and ended it with plastic-covered bump-resistant structures front and rear. The Stingray in the foreground is one of the rare air-conditioned LT-1 cars built late in 1972. The Corvette in the background is a 1977 model.

All three Corvette chief engineers were on hand for the National Corvette Museum's grand opening in Bowling Green, Kentucky, on Labor Day weekend 1994. Dave McLellan (left) joined the late Zora Arkus-Duntov and David Hill in front of a promotional model display. *John Heilig*

see any need to break up the solid-axle years. Once the C5 code became popularized, it was then only natural to retroactively rename the four forerunners: 1953–62 became C1; the Sting Rays of 1963–67, C2; the 1968–82 run, C3; and the 1984–96 cars, C4.

Whatever your count, one thing can't be argued: year in, year out, the Corvette has proved it all night unlike any other car ever sold in any numbers in this country. Its sex appeal has never been questioned, nor imagined. The same goes for its reputation as one of the world's best handling, hottest running fun machines for the money. There have been and still are many world-class sports cars, including Viper, that offer more power and speed. But they also cost many thousands more than Chevrolet's 'glass-bodied babies. Many, many thousands more.

No matter how you slice it, no rival at any price can match the Corvette as far as relative comfort and driver friendliness are concerned. Again, they don't call it "America's only sports car" for nothing. In the beginning, the British sports car ideal encompassed quite a few pains along with its pleasures. Cramped quarters.

Sadly lacking weatherproofing. Untrustworthy mechanicals. Nonexistent creature comforts. Chevrolet's movers and shakers, on the other hand, recognized early on that Yankee car buyers would never put up with such inconveniences. Thus the reasoning behind the addition of conventional exterior door handles, roll-up windows, and an optional removable hardtop to the updated Corvette equation in 1956. Yet another concession to American sensibilities came seven years later in the form of a truly closed coupe body.

The pursuit of perfection has been a major component of the American sports car ideal ever since. But a qualification of terms, however paradoxical at a glance, is required. Perfection in the Corvette's case has always involved a supreme compromise; a balance of things often considered polar opposites. At one end of the scales are all the track-ready features that heat up the blood of a driver familiar with the fast lane. At the other are as many of the commonly taken for granted sedan-like comforts and conveniences that can fit within the two-seater's tight parameters. Of course that balance has always leaned toward the former. But lessons learned and radically improved technologies have since evened out things by bringing the two poles, performance and practicality, much closer together.

Chief engineer David Hill wasn't just bragging in 1997 when he described the C5 as "the best Vette yet." Today's Corvettes are both the hottest to drive at the limit and the coolest to live with in everyday operation. But the same could be said for similar claims made a few decades earlier by Zora Duntov and Dave McLellan. The stunning Sting Ray was indeed the greatest Corvette yet to set tread on American roads in 1963. Some even felt it was more than that. "For the first time I now have a Corvette I can be proud to drive in Europe," said Duntov. McLellan's pride and joy was the redesigned C4 Corvette, *Motor Trend*'s "Car of the Year" for 1984.

In between these two milestone moments in Corvette history came the only model years anyone would dare label as anything less than legendary. Some modern-day critics might even use the word *lackluster*. The longest span of the five generations at 15 years, the C3 run of 1968–82 encompassed both some of the hottest, wildest Corvettes ever built and easily the weakest of the breed. Buyers in 1968 and 1969 could choose between seven different power sources, including the aluminum-head L-89 option for the L-71 427-ci tri-carb big-block. The count in 1969 technically was eight if you added the all-but-unique aluminum ZL-1 427. Outputs in those two years ranged from the standard 300 horses all the way up to the L-71's 435 rompin', stompin' ponies. By 1974, however, only two optional engines were being offered, and the top advertised output had fallen to 270 net-rated horses. Seven years later, all Corvettes sold outside of California were fitted with one engine only, the 190-horse L-81 350 small-block.

Although Corvettes did remain this country's most powerful cars after 1973, that they paled in comparison to their outrageous forerunners left them easy targets for retrospective naysayers. Horsepower-challenged Corvettes of the late 1970s and early 1980s today remain the most overlooked members of Chevrolet's historic, half-century-old performance legacy, especially so from a value-driven collector's standpoint. At best, vintage Corvette dealers

The second-generation "midyear" Corvette run lasted only five years, one more than intended. The first C3 was planned for 1967, but various snafus delayed it a year. In its place came one of the most popular Corvettes of all time, the 1967 Sting Ray.

Like Zora Duntov, GM styling guru Bill Mitchell was among the last of the all-powerful "car guys" to help shape things around General Motors. Mitchell took over from Harley Earl, GM's first great designer, in 1958, then went on to greatness himself. Feathers in his cap included the 1963 Sting Ray, 1968 Corvette, and 1963 Buick Riviera. *Chevrolet Public Relations*

The National Corvette Museum opened across the street from the Corvette assembly plant in Bowling Green, Kentucky, during a massive gala held Labor Day weekend 1994.

The Blue Grass State has been the mecca for the fiberglass faithful since 1981, the year, of course, when Corvette production was transferred east from General Motors' venerable St. Louis facility. The not-so-old Kentucky home to Corvette assembly today is found right off I-65 at exit number 28 on Bowling Green's northeast side. Yankees heading south for the winter can't miss it. Many don't. Nearly 50,000 visitors tour the facility each year. While the plant tour has always drawn a strong and steady stream of Corvette lovers, its popularity has increased noticeably since the C5 was introduced in 1997. It seems that assembling the radically redesigned fifth-generation Corvette has become just as much an attraction as the car itself.

Enhancing exit number 28's attraction even further is the National Corvette Museum, found just as easily across the street from the Bowling Green assembly plant. Passersby truly can't miss this edifice; its bright yellow rotunda topped by the red Mobil 1 Signature Spire, at 11-stories tall, stands as the tallest structure between Louisville and Nashville. The entire complex itself takes up nearly 70,000 square feet on 33 acres, and hopes are to build onto this palace of the past in the near future.

"We will need more room soon, especially for the library," explained Wendell Strode, the NCM's executive director since December 1996. "Within three to five years we'll be running out of space there." That's the good news for Corvette historians and researchers hungry to learn as much as they can about the car of their dreams.

The not-so-good news is that the NCM's prosperity has not matched initial predictions made during the museum's grand opening in September 1994. Strode himself is not shy about admitting the obvious. Public support has not materialized as strongly as the museum's founding fathers envisioned so optimistically earlier in the decade. As the next millennium nears, bringing with it the Corvette's 50th birthday in 2003, NCM people find themselves hustling to find new ways to bolster the NCM's somewhat lukewarm fortunes. According to Strode, about 156,000 people a year have spun the turnstiles over the last 3 years. Nearly 10 years ago, members of the Kentucky Tourism Cabinet claimed that as many as 500,000 Corvette fans would make the trek to Bowling Green each year to visit an automotive valhalla that simply begged to become a reality.

Pioneers including Terry McManmon, Jon Brookmyer, and Ray Battaglini of the National Corvette Restorers Society first began dreaming the dream back in the 1980s. Many others, like former Bowling Green assembly plant human resources manager Darryl Bowlin, quickly joined in, leading to the founding of the National Corvette Museum Foundation in 1988. A temporary home to nearly a half century of Corvette history, the Corvette Museum Annex, opened in downtown Bowling Green in November 1990. In attendance at that opening was the "father of the Corvette" himself, Zora Arkus-Duntov. "Please build this museum and save the things that I've built," was Duntov's plea during his speech.

Two years later, on June 5, 1992, Duntov was at the controls of a one-of-a-kind "Corvette bulldozer" for the National Corvette Museum's ceremonial ground-breaking. Donations of cash, archival materials, even the cars themselves had been arriving in Bowling Green long before that date. Big-time backing for the project came from, among others, General Motors, Chevrolet, Mobil, Goodyear, and the American Sunroof Corporation. About $4 million in private support was supplied by various loyal Corvette owners, parts suppliers, and dealers

worldwide. United Auto Workers members at the Bowling Green plant chipped in $270,000 as well.

The culmination of all that generosity came on Labor Day weekend 1994 in one of the grandest grand openings ever witnessed. Among the 120,000 people who flocked to Bowling Green that weekend were Duntov, Larry Shinoda, Dave McLellan, David Hill, and Jim Perkins, to name just a few of the men behind the machine. Country singer George Jones serenaded luminaries and humble journalists alike during the VIP dinner the night before the ribbon cutting. The Beach Boys were also on hand to do a little harmonizing.

More than 4,000 Corvette owners clicked off about 250,000 miles traveling from points all across the country in 10 Corvette caravans to make it to this big show. Motorists in mere mortal automobiles on I-65 on Saturday morning, September 2, found themselves spit out of luck as police closed down the interstate to through traffic while these caravans wound their way onto the NCM grounds. It was an unforgettable weekend, so much so that museum officials mark it with an annual birthday party every September.

But some onlookers were soon left wondering just how many birthdays lay ahead not long after the Beach Boys packed up their surfboards and went home. Financial difficulties quickly arose, due partly to the museum board's inexperience in such matters as fund-raising, banking, and corporate relations. The founding fathers themselves were the first to admit that they were basically "just a bunch of Corvette guys." That those guys managed to transform their dream into a reality is a testament to their steadfast dedication. Keeping that dream alive, however, has proven to be a much higher hurdle, a task requiring sure-handed management. Even Dan Gale, the driving force behind the museum's opening, admitted that "we made a bunch of mistakes."

A solution to the problem involved turning to professional help. When Wendell Strode arrived in late 1996, he brought along 25 years of banking experience—that, and he's a died-in-the-wool Corvette guy, too.

Among Strode's first goals was to restore credibility with everyone: GM, bankers, sponsors, and Corvette lovers themselves. He was amazed to find a chasm growing between the museum and the Corvette guys and gals who should be, in his

mind, the NCM's main source of support. Foundation membership was shrinking, and it was this trend that Strode felt he had to reverse first in order to get things back on track. The museum would never survive without growth. And according to Strode, "the key to such growth is the membership. Corvette people have to love this place." Since Strode arrived the foundation roll call has increased from 1,600 to 4,000. "Membership is on the rise," he said, "but of course I would like to see more."

Strode's plans for future growth also involve adding "second-season exhibits," displays created with "more casual visitors" in mind. Meant to entice non-Corvette people through the turnstiles during slower times, these exhibits feature fun topics like dinosaurs and NASA-related activities. General car shows are also planned for a summertime schedule already full of Corvette-related gatherings. To that end, 25 additional acres adjacent to NCM property were purchased in November 1998 to make room for more parking.

Among Strode's top goals today is the library, which remained incomplete five years after the museum's grand opening due to Chevrolet officials' hesitancy to donate records, build sheets, and such. It was left up to the NCM team to prove that their facility could indeed adequately house and securely preserve the material. That proof can now be found in the present growth nurtured by Strode and his staff.

As Wendell Strode says, the rest is up to you. The future of one of the finest automotive museums in the country depends on your support. If you would like to make a difference—simply a visit would be a start—call the National Corvette Museum at (502) 781-7973 for information. Web surfers should check in at *www.corvettemuseum.com* for all the latest news.

One of the two 1969 ZL-1 Corvettes built (this one owned by Roger Judski) is shown here while on display in December 1997. Next to the car is an all-aluminum ZL-1 427 V-8.

Sculptor Karen Atta cast more than 20 statues of some of the great men who made Corvette history. You decide which is the real Dave McLellan. Dave and his likeness were on hand for the VIP party the night before the NCM's ribbon-cutting ceremony.

consider these underpriced relics as little more than affordable, entry-level opportunities for less wealthy Corvette crazies to join the fiberglass fraternity.

Clearly, as far as investment opportunity is concerned, the bulk of the C3 generation rank among the least desired Corvettes of all-time. At the same time, casual history too seemingly ignores this group. Enthusiast clubs across the country that use the label "Classic Corvette" always cut memberships off at the knees at 1967, almost as if Chevrolet stopped building fiberglass two-seaters then. Granted, the so-called "midyear" models of 1963–67 deserve their status as the easiest recognized, most popular vintage Corvettes out there. But is it fair that the C3s, affectionately known as "Sharks" by Corvette followers who refuse to turn a blind eye, be forever lost in the giant shadow cast by the original Sting Ray?

It remains difficult, of course, to completely overlook the C3 cars, what with such luminaries as the L-88s of 1968–69, the 1969 ZL-1, the LS-6 454 big-block of 1971, and the LT-1 small-blocks of 1970–72 present and well accounted for. On the flipside, however, other historic milestones posted during the third-generation run tended to signal that what once was, might never be again. The last big-block Corvette was built in 1974. The last convertible (for the moment) came a year later. The fabled "Stingray" badge (made one word after its return to Corvette flanks in 1969 following a one-year hiatus) was last used in 1976. On a lesser note, conventional chromed bumpers began to disappear in 1973 as the car's nose went the monochromatic, 5-mile-per-hour crash resistant route. The tail then followed suit in 1974.

A changing of the guard also occurred in 1975 as Zora Duntov retired in January. Dave McLellan then became the Corvette's second chief engineer. Another legendary figure, William Mitchell, traded his powerful perch atop GM Styling for the golf course in 1977 after 19 years of essentially single-handedly deciding the future face of the next year's Corvette. The fate of America's only sports car would never again hinge on the will of any one man, however strong, after Mitchell's departure. McLellan, Hill, Chuck Jordan, Jerry Palmer—although Jordan might disagree, none of these top players in the C4/C5 game came close to matching the individual impacts

made by Mitchell and certainly Duntov in their heydays.

Revisionist historians and exploitative entrepreneurs might look disparagingly at the C3 editions today, but in their own heydays the cars themselves did quite well for themselves, thank you. Sales were by no means lackluster. The first Shark in 1968 established a new production high of 28,566 coupes and convertibles, breaking the previous record of 27,720 set in 1966. The 1969 Corvette then became the first to surpass 30,000 in annual sales on the way to a new all-time high of 38,762 cars. Of course it should be mentioned that newly appointed Chevrolet chief John DeLorean allowed the 1969 model run to work overtime into December after a strike delayed production for two months early in the year. This in turn restricted 1970's effort, resulting in a drop to 17,316 Corvettes.

From there, sales increased each year up through 1977. Total production for 1973 again reached the 30,000 plateau, a first as far as a regulation 12-month model run was concerned. As it was, 1969's "asterisk" was finally rendered moot in 1976 when the 40,000 barrier was breached. Now made up of coupes only, 1976's new sales standard totaled out at 46,558. Yet another record, one that still stands, was established in 1979 as sales surpassed 50,000 for the first time. The final tally for 1979 was 53,807.

So what's up with that? How could these cars be so popular then, yet so easily overlooked today? One answer involves the basic law of supply and demand. All that supply may have made Chevrolet beancounters happy a quarter-century ago, but it also naturally hindered nostalgic demand later on. Why would anyone have worried about preserving one of these babies for the ages when there were so damned many of them around?

Resale values in turn suffered from the outset. C3 models stuck around on used car lots, wearing unaccustomed used car price tags, far longer than any other Corvette breed. Some occasionally can still be found there with soaped-up windshields even today. Why even consider restoring a later C3 when you'd spend far more green than anyone would ever pay for the final product?

Many critics, cruel or otherwise, also feel that the C3's apparent popularity in the 1970s didn't exactly reflect reality. Forget for the moment that the third-generation Corvette ran up against certainly the heaviest odds ever faced by its creators: stumbling blocks included

Dave McLellan's team bid a fond farewell to the C3 in 1982 by putting together the classy Collectors Edition package. David Hill's crew pulled off a similar trick with a Collectors Edition model of their own (background) to mark the last C4 Corvette in 1996.

The C3 was basically a rebodied midyear Corvette. Initially, the third-generation chassis with its independent rear suspension carried over unchanged from the 1963 Sting Ray, shown here. Standard four-wheel disc brakes were added in 1965. *Chevrolet Motor Division*

C3 Corvettes are lovingly known as "Sharks." That nickname dates back to the Shark showcar of 1961, which was later renamed Mako Shark I after the Mako Shark II appeared in 1965. The Mako Shark II body showcased the shape that would become the production Corvette in 1968.

Shark by Chevrolet—ACtion sparked by AC

The same AC Spark Plugs that add power to this car of tomorrow are available for your car today! Engineers specify ACs for experimental cars like the Corvette Shark because of AC's self-cleaning Hot Tip. It heats faster to burn away fouling carbon deposits — delivers longer peak power — greater economy for every car! Don't experiment with your spark plugs, ask for ACtion . . . ask for AC.

AC
FIRE-RING
SPARK PLUGS

Dave McLellan (at left) took over control of the Corvette's future after Zora Duntov retired in January 1975. His impact was first felt in 1978 when a new "fastback" rear-end treatment debuted. With a 1978 Indy Pace Car replica and the Corvette's second chief engineer here are Chevrolet general manager Robert Lund (far right) and GM exec Robert Stempel (second from right). *Chevrolet Motor Division*

the emergence of ever-tightening government-mandated emissions standards and safety regulations in 1968; soaring insurance rates for performance cars during the period of 1969–72; skyrocketing gasoline prices resulting from the 1973 energy crisis; another federal mandate, this one specifying new fuel economy standards in 1978; even higher gas prices; and a national economic disaster in 1979. All that aside, more than one armchair historian has concluded that the C3 breed deserves little relative respect today because much of the attention it received 25 years ago came by way of mirrors. Sure, those record production figures seemingly said that Americans then couldn't get enough of Chevrolet's fiberglass two-seater. Those numbers, however, were apparently part of a mirage. Perhaps Chevy wouldn't have sold nearly as many Corvettes in the decade's latter half had not nearly all the competition retired from the race.

All-American horsepower was all but dead by 1973, a victim of changing times. Hemi Mopars, Super Cobra Jet Fords, and all the other ultra-high-performance big-block machines saw their last days in 1971, the year

OFFICIAL PACE CAR
62nd ANNUAL INDIANAPOLIS 500 MILE RACE
MAY 28, 1978

when automakers radically slashed engine compression as part of a federally mandated detuning plan aimed at cleaning up Detroit's internal combustion act. Although a few steadfast survivors, mostly from Pontiac, held out to the very last breath in 1972, 1973, and 1974, the breed known as America's musclecar died a quick death as the environmentally conscious 1970s dawned.

While major price differentials set Corvettes and musclecars well apart as far as direct competition was concerned, the two forms of fast transportation still shared the same segment of the car-buying market. And that piece of the pie was soon sliced down to almost nothing in the 1970s. By 1973, performance-minded buyers could pick from two plums: Pontiac's Trans Am and Chevrolet's Corvette. Like the Corvette, the more affordable Trans Am also experienced a sales spike in the 1970s, this one even more dramatic. Production soared from 4,800 in 1973 to more than 117,000 six years later. Clearly both cars benefited greatly from the "captive audience" left searching for ways to satisfy their need for speed after the musclecar's demise.

In the Corvette's case, that 1970s sales spike also featured a downside that helped trigger additional slings and arrows. Setting and resetting sales records increased both revenues and quality control maladies. Chevrolet had had a hard enough time consistently molding and painting the midyear Sting Rays to high enough standards, and this was at an average production rate of about 20,000 cars a year. Raising that rate by half, then doubling it only helped make matters worse. Complaints about poor fitting, wavy panels and "orange-peel" paint surfaced immediately in 1968 and could be heard throughout the C3 run.

But also heard were comments most bystanders today seem to have forgotten. When *Car and Driver* tested the new "soft-nosed" 1973 Corvette, not one whine about diminishing horsepower was printed. "Zora Arkus-Duntov reckons the new Corvette to be the best ever," read *Car and Driver*'s December 1972 report. "And after exhaustive testing of four different models, we're inclined to agree."

Sound familiar? Even with less-than-perfect bodywork and ever-weakening engines, the C3 models were still Corvettes. And Corvettes have never been anything less than kings of the hill—for nearly 50 years now.

Long live the king.

Chevrolet's St. Louis assembly plant was home to Corvette production from December 1953 to July 1981. The Fisher Mill Building, located in the far upper left corner of the complex (behind the white water tower to the left of the smokestack), housed the Corvette assembly line. *St. Louis Mercantile Library*

Various strikes hindered GM production efforts in the late 1960s and 1970s. The three picketeers shown here were among 8,100 employees idled by a strike at the St. Louis plant that began April 10, 1969. Corvette production that year ran into overtime (it ended in December) due to such delays. *St. Louis Mercantile Library*

17

Chapter 1

SHARK SIGHTINGS
Development of the Third-Generation Corvette

The Corvette, like your best girlfriend in high school, has never been able to make it downstairs on time for the big date. Consider the C5. Early hopes around Chevrolet in the late 1980s had an all-new fifth-generation Corvette debuting in time for the car's 40th birthday bash. That meant 1993. Then along came various trials and tribulations, not the least of which was General Motors' red ink bath in the early 1990s. The proposed delivery date slipped to 1994. Then 1995. Then 1996. Before we knew it the project was all but dead. Fortunately a rebirth followed, resulting in the long-awaited C5's introduction in January 1997. All was forgiven.

Similar tales, with far fewer chapters, were written earlier each time the best Vette yet stood poised to make its anticipated appearance. Who can forget 1983? Chevrolet did, this after ever-present gremlins helped push the C4's planned debut back more than six months. The C3's record run finally ended in 1982. The comparably lengthy C4 stretch began with the 1984 model. How time flies when you're having fun following fiberglass futures.

Twenty-five years before, the rumor mill had the public anxiously awaiting a radically redesigned Corvette for 1960. In this case a perceived tease was probably more the result of premature press predictions than any real stumbling or bumbling on GM's part. Chevrolet simply would sell no Sting Ray before its time. That moment arrived in 1963, and anyone with eyes agreed the results were well worth the wait. No question about it, this was the best 'Vette yet.

But then Duntov and crew found themselves seemingly painted into a corner. How do you top a classic? And how much time should you take trying? The solid-axle Corvette had carried on for 10 years, much longer, in many critics' minds, than it should have—thus the 1960 prophecies. Chevrolet's braintrust apparently agreed, or at least they recognized that Sting Ray customers were bound to begin wondering, "What have you done for me lately?"

The second-generation Corvette's days became numbered almost as quickly as they began. Duntov and Bill Mitchell began independently brainstorming new ideas concerning the Corvette's next move even before the original Sting Ray's well-earned raves died out. A legend in its own time or not, the midyear models would be history by the fall of 1966. Four years and out was the plan, as was topping a classic—literally. The original Sting Ray had already pushed retooling costs to the limit with its independently suspended chassis and reinforced, restyled bodyshell. Busting the bank again only a few years down the road was out of the question. The bulk of the job of building the third-generation Corvette was then left to Mitchell as a new body atop the existing platform was planned. For 1967.

Luckily for midyear worshippers, that plan typically did not end up in the best-laid category.

As always, improving performance was Duntov's prime goal. And this time he desperately

Designer Larry Shinoda's touch is clearly evident in the lines of the rear-engined XP-819, which was first conceived by R&D man Frank Winchell in 1964.

Various XP-819 features, such as the one-piece lift-off roof and inner-door steel guard beams, foretold later Corvette developments. That fat tail hinged upward to reveal a small-block V-8 perched backward, Corvair-style, behind the rear wheels.

wanted to concentrate on one particularly disappointing aspect of the second-generation Corvette's go-fast personality. A *Car and Driver* report later in 1971 described "the contempt Duntov feels for the body shape of the 1963–1967 Sting Ray." In Zora's own words, that body possessed "just enough lift to be a bad airplane." Duntov's Grand Sport racers of 1963 never had a chance of keeping pace with the world's best sports cars due to, among other things, their inherent preference to take flight instead of sticking to the track. That his Grand Sport project was abruptly cancelled by GM executive office decree only spared Zora and the Corvette additional embarrassment on the international stage.

Designer Larry Shinoda, Mitchell's right-hand man, described the situation to *Corvette Fever* contributor Don Sherman in 1989. "GM wind-tunnel engineers attempting to justify their theories spent untold sums studying the 1963 Corvette," said Shinoda. "What they found was a drag coefficient of 0.53. In essence, it was a flying machine."

Of course aerodynamic automotive design was still not exactly a science in the 1960s, certainly not to the degree it is today. John Cafaro's C5 design team three decades later was totally dedicated to transforming the latest, greatest Corvette into the slickest shape ever to slip out of not only Bowling Green, but Detroit too. Cafaro achieved the 1997 Corvette's unprecedented

XP-819's inner door panels serve double duty (when closed) as a side bolster for the tight-fitting bucket seats. The label on the dash reads "Dev. Car See Nies." Larry Nies was the engineer responsible for the car's unique rear-engine design.

0.29 drag coefficent by doing what the wind tunnel told him to do, and this meant sticking with an aspect of the tunnel-tested shape that drew the most negative comments at unveiling time—the car's sharp-edged, flat-backed tail.

"That is there specifically for aerodynamics," said Kurt Romberg, the engineer responsible for the C5's abrupt ending. "We spent a lot of time locating that hard edge, and what it does is it separates the air cleanly off the car." The newest Corvette couldn't top out at a definitely world-class 180 miles per hour without that clean cut. Style-conscious critics may have cringed, but clearly the days of form following function have been replaced with function dictating form.

It was thoughts to the opposite that primarily dictated styling decisions in Bill Mitchell's day. In the 1960s, looking like the wind was a friend remained a much more important priority than actually cutting through the air with precision. Mitchell had already proven himself more than willing to place form well ahead of function before work on the C3 began—witness the visibility-inhibiting "stinger" that split the 1963 Sting Ray coupe's rear window in two. Duntov knew that one would never fly for long and tried to remove it, but Mitchell was adamant. "If you take that off, you might as well forget the whole thing," he snorted.

That's not to say that Mitchell was totally blind to the importance of a fully functional Corvette form. He was no fu-fu designer walled up in an ivory tower studio far from the realities experienced by his designs. He was a certified car nut, with one of his many favorite sayings (borrowed in part from his mentor, Harley Earl) being "you've gotta have gasoline in your veins to be a real car designer." He was also a speed freak who loved his Corvettes to be of the balls-out, full-race variety—witness his 1956 SR-2 and 1959 Stingray.

"From the time that Bill started driving sports cars, he has never taken his foot off the gas," wrote fellow designer Strother MacMinn in *Automobile Quarterly* in 1988. Said Mitchell in 1984, "As long as there's a Corvette on four wheels, a hot bike on two, that I can do something with, I'll stay young." Yes, Bill Mitchell was a lead-footed gearhead, one of the last truly great "car guys" to rule with heart and soul in Detroit. Yet he was a style-conscious designer first, and it was fashion that governed his hand.

"When they were doing the [C3]," he told *Automobile Quarterly*, "I went down there, and it was all square-cornered, and I put on an act and said, 'We're never going to do a box around my place.' I wanted it to look like it was born in a wind tunnel." Even though he actually used the term *wind tunnel*, he was basically only

The first Mako Shark II showcar was a nonrunning mockup featuring dummy side exhausts. The "Mark IV 396" badges on the hood scoop were also dummies—there was no engine, big- or small-block, beneath the hood. *Chevrolet Motor Division*

concerned with creating an analogy. The key words here were *look like*. Appearances and impressions were always his top priorities.

A boxy, brick-shaped Corvette was not his bag primarily because it didn't look good, and in Mitchell's own words, "If it doesn't look good, why bother getting in?" Many of his famous one-liners resulted from his apparent belief that it was better to look good than to feel good: "Barrymore's nose is better looking than Churchill's." "A collie is better looking than a bulldog." "A shark looks better than a grouper."

That latter profundity also related to another of Mitchell's pet preferences. He was especially fond of aggressive sea creatures—stingrays, for example. He kept a stuffed mako shark on his studio wall, and its graduated toning intrigued him, so much so that he demanded that the XP-755 showcar be finished to match. Created in 1961, XP-755 showcased much of the up-

coming 1963 Sting Ray's look. But it didn't start showing off that look until it was finally painted, and that took some doing. As the oft-told legend has it, Mitchell continually rejected the paint crew's futile efforts to match the shark's natural shadings. The O.K. was finally given only after painters sneaked into Mitchell's office one night and colored the fish to match the car. Believe it or not.

XP-755, of course, then became the Shark, and therein lies the origins of the third-generation Corvette's pet name. A second showcar, the Mako Shark, appeared in 1965. Not long after its birth, the Mako Shark was rechristened Mako Shark II as XP-755 was retroactively renamed Mako Shark I. And just as XP-755 foretold the Sting Ray's arrival, so too did the Mako Shark II allow show-goers at least a partial look at the C3 Corvette—which, remember, was promised for 1967.

Transforming the Mako Shark II image into reality, however, proved more difficult than expected. Function truly suffered with this form as driver visibility, engine ventilation and, yes, aerodynamics fell well below acceptable standards. Per Mitchell's prerogative, the prototype Shark shape looked great. But it functioned more like a flying fish as unwanted lift again proved to be a troublesome hitch. Duntov found himself forced to push the C3's introduction back a year while these problems were ironed out. In the meantime, one more midyear Sting Ray was rolled back out for 1967—an unintended encore, if you will. That car, as fate would have it, has since attained its own legendary status. Sometimes the worst-laid plans end up the best.

Delaying the C3's introduction by a year not only allowed the 1967 Sting Ray a chance at immortality, it also gave Duntov the time to deal with bugs as best he could, which he found himself doing right up to the 1968 Corvette's press introduction. But that's not to say that Zora played the hero to Mitchell's goat. Not at all. Mitchell simply did his job, Duntov did his. New model development back then wasn't anywhere near as integrated as it is today. As Larry Shinoda wrote in *Shark Quarterly* in 1997, "Bill and Zora didn't agree on the design at first. But this was in the era when design came first and engineering then got to work within the major parameters we set."

People may have listened when Duntov spoke, but Mitchell clearly was no stranger to having the last word concerning the Corvette. And as much as it appeared that some of his demands and directions proved to be more trouble than they were worth, his contributions to the Corvette legacy remain every bit as legendary as Zora's.

According to Henry Haga, who headed the Chevrolet 2 studio where the final C3 form was fashioned, Mitchell was "the Corvette's most important ally at GM." "In Bill's influence, those of us in the design studios had something to guide us: his feeling of what the Corvette should be," continued Haga in *Corvette: The Legend Lives On*. "He had a facility for setting a trend that you could put into production. That's what was so great about Bill, he had the foresight to leap out and do show cars and production cars that needed doing. In a world where there was no Mako Shark and no Sting Ray, he suddenly made them."

Of course he didn't make them without help. Overseeing Henry Haga and his Chevy 2 gang during Shark development was Chevrolet chief stylist David Holls. Larry Shinoda was head of the mysterious Chevrolet 3 studio in 1965 and 1966. Chevy 3 became known as "the warehouse" because it was hidden away in a GM Styling storage building on the Tech Center's south side. Among the stylists who worked there with Shinoda was John Schinella, who later went on to head GM's Advanced Concepts Center in Southern California. In 1990, Schinella's Advanced Concepts team created the sensational Sting Ray III showcar, a stepping stone of sorts to the C5. In 1965, Schinella assisted Shinoda with the C3's stepping stone, the Mako Shark II. Chevrolet 3 was also the home to the earliest C3 prototype theme, which Shinoda then passed on to Haga at Chevrolet 2 for final refinements on the way to production.

Watching over it all—design and engineering—was Elliott "Pete" Estes, who had filled the vacated general manager's seat at Chevrolet in 1965 after Semon "Bunkie" Knudsen left to climb the GM corporate ladder. Like Knudsen prior to 1961, Estes had previously held the reins at Pontiac. Also like Bunkie, Pete was no stranger to the fast lane, he being the mover and shaker who had had the foresight to shepherd the supposedly taboo GTO through GM red tape into production in 1964. As was often the case when a new face arrived atop a GM division, Estes' move to Chevrolet helped open the door to fresh ideas, as well as the possible rethinking of earlier proposals shot down by the previous regime. The time was ripe to create the next new Corvette.

One of the earliest steps toward this creation actually came before Estes' arrival by way of a long-forgotten engineering presentation made by Duntov to Bunkie Knudsen in April 1964. Zora's initial premise in this presentation involved the obvious fact that the 1965 Corvette would be wearing the identical body seen in 1963 and 1964. This, in his learned opinion, could not continue if Knudsen expected America's only sports car to stay out in front ahead of the times. At the least, Duntov wanted a rebody for 1966. At most, he asked for a totally re-engineered Corvette for 1967.

Included in his proposal was a relatively mild facelift for 1966, an estimated $5 million upgrade that didn't differ all that much from the

The second Mako Shark II built was a fully functional model without sidepipes. This time beneath the hood was the 427 big-block, which was just then being readied for use in production Corvettes for 1966. *Chevrolet Motor Division*

existing Sting Ray. He also pitched another radical race car, the GS 3, with the two letters being short for "Grand Sport." Duntov wanted to build 10 Grand Sport 3 racers in 1966 at a cost of $1.125 million. These machines would closely resemble the mid-engined, all-wheel-drive CERV II and would be used to promote Chevrolet engineering advances at the track.

More radical were the two production alternatives he proposed for 1967. Both offered significant weight cuts by way of a stronger, yet lighter frame featuring a central tunnel "backbone." And each wore completely modernized bodies. But while one of these 1967 proposals was of conventional design with the engine in front, the other, like the CERV II, would mount its engine amidships between the driver and rear wheels. Rough cost estimates were $20 million for the former, $38.5 million for the latter. Projected curb weights for the two were 2,200 pounds for the front-engined proposal, 2,475 for the midshipman.

While keeping the Corvette's weight in line was always one of Duntov's top priorites, so too was balancing that weight. He was well

aware of the importance of weight bias long before he joined Chevrolet's engineering team in May 1953. Getting the bulk of a car's poundage off the front wheels has always been one of the main keys to maximizing road-handling capabilities. Doing so, however, has never been an easy task with a big V-8 mounted up front in typical American style.

Moving the transmission to the rear—like engineers in the 1990s did for the C5—to reduce the forward weight bias was considered as early as 1957 for the "Q-Corvette" project, which foretold the 1963 Sting Ray. It was considered, but never put into development. However, the mid-engined CERV I engineering practice was. It appeared in 1960, and then was followed by the CERV II four years later. Although Duntov's April 1964 midengined proposal never made it beyond the drawing board stage (nor did his 1966 makeover), various other engine relocation plans did. And not all stopped at the midengine ideal.

Frank Winchell's research and development team hastily put together the XP-819 Corvette in 1964. At the time, many minds around GM had high hopes for a high-perform-ance variation on the rear-engined Corvair platform. Winchell had even gone so far as to build a V-8-powered Corvair prototype, a layout he felt might also work well beneath the Corvette's skin.

Duntov, however, never did like Winchell's rear-engined Corvette idea, especially so after initial drawings appeared downright ugly. Enter the ever-present Larry Shinoda. Shinoda had already drawn up the XP-755 Shark, Mitchell's Stingray, the production Sting Ray, and CERVs I and II, to name a few. Now he was promising he could make Winchell's idea work in pleasing fashion. "Where did you cheat?" asked a sur-prised Duntov upon seeing Shinoda's sketches.

Taking XP-819 from paper to fiberglass amazingly required only a few months. Engineer Larry Nies' team built a backbone chassis with independent coils at the corners. Wheelbase was a stubby 90 inches. In back, Nies suspended an alloy 287-ci V-8 rearward off a modified Pon-tiac Tempest automatic transaxle. Seventy per-cent of XP-819's 2,700 pounds rested on the rear tires, which were super-wide Firestones.

Despite Shinoda's claim that all that rubber helped compensate for XP-819's radical rear-ward weight bias, other witnesses weren't so sure. According to automotive journalist and former Chevrolet engineer Paul Van Valken-burgh, "The car could be set up to handle prop-erly on a skid pad in steady-state cornering, but transient or dynamic response was nearly un-controllable at the limit." Rolling proof of Van Valkenburgh's conclusion came when XP-819 careened into a guard rail during testing. So much for the rear-engine idea.

Much more significant to the continuing Corvette legacy was the XP-819's shell. Shaped by Shinoda and Schinella, its "Coke-bottle" body introduced many elements that would later show up in the third-generation Corvette via the Mako Shark II. The low, pointed nose. Those high wheel bulges. That ducktailed rear. Guard beams inside XP-819's doors also pre-dicted a Shark feature, as did the tunneled rear window. The urethane body-colored front bumper foretold a Corvette upgrade to come in 1973. The one-piece lift-off roof did the same for a comparable top design unveiled along with the new C4 for 1984.

Few witnesses noticed XP-819's prophecies however, as it was shuffled off into history as

quickly as it had arrived on the scene. And soon after it was gone, Shinoda and Schinella turned their attentions toward the car that nearly everyone predicted would become the next new Corvette.

Bill Mitchell first laid down the law con-cerning this machine to Shinoda's team midway in 1964. Mitchell's specifications included a coupe body with a "pinched" center section ala that "Coke-bottle" trend. The wheels would be prominently displayed with fender areas that appeared well-defined yet fully integrated into the body. The low, low roof too would be melded into that slim center section so it wouldn't look like a separate top tacked onto a convertible. A tapered tail in the best tradition of the original Sting Ray coupe would end things. Per Mitchell's mandate, all this futuristic fashion would have to fit on the existing Corvette chas-sis—with its engine up front. And the whole works would have to be fully fashioned in time

The Mako Shark II's 427 V-8 was fitted with an air-conditioning compressor and the newly introduced Turbo Hydra-Matic automatic transmission. Turbo Hydra-Matic didn't become a Corvette option until 1968. *Chevrolet Motor Division*

Drawing On Experience

Zora Arkus-Duntov was, of course, "the father of the Corvette." It didn't matter that he wasn't even around when conception occurred. Nor does saying this represent a slight to the many other proud father figures. Duntov deserves such an honor because it was he above any other who helped steer the car away from an early demise in 1955 into the history books. "The greatest of the Corvette prophets," as *Corvette Fever* called him in 1999, was being revered as highly as his beloved two-seat babies even before his retirement in 1975. "Zora Arkus-Duntov is so firmly identified with Corvettes they could bear his name," wrote *Car and Driver*'s Jan Norbye in 1962. Most of history's prime movers and shakers have to wait until after their deaths to attain mythical stature. Duntov's legend, on the other hand, was looming larger than life long before his mortal presence left this world for the next on April 21, 1996.

That Zora still casts a giant shadow goes without saying. It is so large it all but obscures many of the other great names associated with the half-century-old Corvette legacy. One of the more prominent entries on that list, at least from a Shark fan's perspective, reads "Shinoda."

A legend in his own right, veteran designer Lawrence Kiyoshi Shinoda knew more than a little about the short end of the stick. He was an 11-year-old Nisei child growing up in southern California when Pearl Harbor was attacked on December 7, 1941, meaning he and his Japanese-American family were then locked up in the Manzanar interment camp. Ironically, he later served with the Air National Guard in Korea.

Shinoda had the unfortunate honor of working under another of GM's larger-than-life giants, Bill Mitchell. What Duntov was to Corvette engineering, Mitchell was to Sting Ray styling. Same for the Shark. Although Zora had a lot to say about what did or didn't fly, Mitchell was certainly no slouch when it came to throwing his weight around. And he was also more than willing to accept all the kudos for the new Corvette bodies unveiled in 1963 and 1968. Sure, it was Mitchell who rode herd over Corvette styling in the 1960s. It was he who supplied the direction and decision-making. But it was Larry Shinoda who first put it on paper.

A few decades passed and Shinoda found himself pushed aside by history again as the fiberglass faithful flocked to praise the almighty father in his waning years. Being overshadowed, however, was something an aging Shinoda never did accept. His dissenting opinions concerning Duntov's dominance of the nostalgic limelight were openly expressed more than once during the 1990s.

"He was the Don Rickles of the design world, a colorful individual who spoke his mind and occasionally ruffled the wrong feathers," wrote good friend and *Sports Car International* editor

Larry Shinoda worked for both Ford and Chevrolet in his younger years, and he had the unique honor of creating images for two arch-rivals, Ford's Boss 302 Mustang and Chevy's Z/28 Camaro. Shinoda was caught on film here during the VIP dinner held the night before the National Corvette Museum's grand opening in September 1994.

D. Randy Riggs following Shinoda's death on November 13, 1997. "But that was why I admired him—there wasn't a phony bone in his body. He was our kind of car guy."

Shinoda never liked taking a backseat to anyone, which explains why he was such a demon behind the wheel. A red-blooded American hot-rodder from the day he received his license in 1946, his need for speed drove him to various victories at various competition venues in the 1950s. His 1929 Ford Hi-boy, the "Chopsticks Special," scored a class record at Bonneville. He also set records on National Hot Rod Association drag strips.

Shinoda was a familiar face around Indianapolis as well. He was a pit crewman for the Indy 500 winner four times. And he also designed the paint scheme for Pat Flaherty's 1956 Indy champ.

His competitive—make that rebellious—spirit also helped explain why he didn't eventually climb the corporate ladder in Detroit. "He's brilliant, but he's also an outspoken maverick," wrote *Automobile's* David E. Davis Jr., 20 years ago while running the show at *Car and Driver*. "Anytime the emperor walked into Shinoda's studio without any clothes on, Shinoda made sure he knew he was naked. This sort of honesty does not augur well for long-term success in Detroit, where the proper team spirit in committee work will get you a lot further than charismatic candor. Whatever else history may say about Lawrence K. Shinoda in years hence, it'll never call him a great committee man."

After leaving the Art Center College of Design in Pasadena early—for being "a malcontent," in his words—Shinoda went to work first for Ford in 1955, Packard in 1956, GM from late 1956 to 1968, then Ford again for another short stint. He designed trucks briefly for White and International Harvester in the 1970s, then opened his own studio.

Along with the 1963 Sting Ray, Shinoda's long design resumé included everything from motorcycles, to custom wheels, to the Goodyear blimp. As he told *Motor Trend* in 1973, he didn't want to be remembered "just as the designer who could design show cars.

"The way I look at it is that a designer should be able to design a tractor, a motor home, or anything on wheels, not just wild-looking sports cars," continued Shinoda. "That's basically what a good industrial designer is. He can do any job that comes."

Maybe so, but he is still remembered best for the dream machines he drew up while at Chevrolet. Among the more prominent were Bill Mitchell's Stingray race car, the CERV I and II experimentals, Jim Hall's Chaparral 2C and 2D racers, Mako Sharks I and II, and the Corvair Super Spyder, Monza GT, and Monza SS showcars.

After following fellow GM defector Bunkie Knudsen to Ford in 1968, Shinoda also found himself working on the rival to a potent Chevy product he had helped promote earlier. He supplied the images for both the original Z/28 Camaro and its main Trans-Am competitor, Ford's Boss 302 Mustang. Henry Ford II then rewarded Larry for the latter by firing him, along with Knudsen, late in 1969. When asked later what he thought of corporate life in Dearborn, he said, "you could call it conservative, or you could call it some other things too. They had a strange way of doing things."

Shinoda's way of doing things was always the aggressive way. Taking no for an answer was never his style. After futilely waiting four days in GM offices for an initial interview in 1956, he finally managed to attract the attention of the fin man himself, Harley Earl. Impressed with the young designer's portfolio, Earl asked Shinoda about salary requirements. As he later said in Don Sherman's 1989 *Corvette Fever* interview, "I quickly tacked $200 per month on to what I earned at Packard. Earl rounded the amount of $200 per month higher still and asked when I could report to work."

He did so on September 15, 1956, the same day another Packard refugee, John DeLorean, came onboard at GM. Shinoda then became Mitchell's favored son of sorts after going to work on big Bill's "private racer," the Stingray, in the winter of 1958. From there followed the first Shark, the production Sting Ray, and the Mako Shark II.

Larry Shinoda was awaiting a kidney transplant when he died at age 67. Perhaps now his name will become the stuff of legends.

Shinoda's eye-catching automotive drawings were most often easily recognized by their contour line "grids." This is an early rendition of the CERV I race car, built in 1959.

The Mako Shark II was restyled into the Manta Ray showcar in 1969. A chin spoiler up front and a lengthened, tapered tail were among modifications made that year. *Courtesy Automobile Quarterly*

for New York's International Auto Show, scheduled for April 1965.

No problem.

A nonrunning full-size mockup was rolled out for press release photography in March—rolled out because even though the hood said "Mark IV 396," there was no such thing residing beneath. Originally labeled Mako Shark, as mentioned, its badging had become Mako Shark II after it was decided to convince the public that this was the second in a series of showcars that meant business. Like the XP-755 Shark, which was now the Mako Shark I, the Mako Shark II was very much a prototype. As Pete Estes explained early in 1965, "the reaction of people who view this car during the next few months could very well influence future design decisions." Added *Hot Rod*'s Eric Dahlqist, "let's hope Chevrolet's Special Engineering boys land this one by 1967." At the

same time a *Car Life* headline asked, is this the "next Corvette?"

The car in question was a second, fully functional Mako Shark II. This one actually was fitted with Chevrolet's newly introduced Mk IV big-block V-8, only the displacement was 427 cubic inches, not 396. Swapping engines (or in this case, putting an engine where there wasn't one before) represented just one of many adjustments made during the Mako Shark II's crowd-pleasing run on the auto show stage.

Show-goers in April 1965 couldn't have cared less that the original Mako mockup didn't have an engine. It looked fast enough while standing still. "As an overall design it kind of fills the mental outlines of the car Cato always had ready in that seemingly abandoned warehouse for the Green Hornet to rocket off into the night," wrote *Hot Rod*'s Eric Dahlquist in 1965.

A sharply pointed prow led the way, followed by a domed hood that signified power. Bulging wheelhouses at all four corners looked ready to explode, their flared openings barely able to contain the fat Firestones (8.80x15 up front, 9.15x15 in back) found within. The aluminum wheels were similar to the 1967 Sting Ray's optional "knockoffs," but, at 7.5 inches, were much wider.

Adding to the "zoomy" image were cast-aluminum side exhausts that exited the empty engine room halfway up the front fenders. These finned side pipes were painted in crackle black with the edges of the fins remaining polished bright. The paint was later removed after the New York showing and the pipes were fully polished. Side exhausts were then deleted altogether on the second Mako Shark II once its 427 big-block went in place.

Original impressions were both bold and beautiful. Body edges were sharp while contours were seductively soft. Measuring 3 inches lower than the existing Sting Ray's profile, the Mako's definitely integrated roofline rolled back into a tapered exclamation point made even more boldfaced by six window louvers that could be opened or closed electrically. The top itself was hinged at the rear, allowing it to flip open to improve access to the clearly cramped quarters below. A pronounced ducktail brought up the rear. And of course the whole package was painted dark down to light (Firefrost Midnight Blue, to lighter blue, to light gray) to match Mitchell's stuffed shark. Or vice versa.

Inside, the Mako Shark II's seats were fixed. As was the case at the feet of XP-819 drivers, the Mako's footpedals adjusted electrically to and fro. Equally unconventional was the aircraft-style steering wheel, which looked like a rectangle squeezed in slightly on the bottom. Incorporated into the wheel's top horizontal bar were two thumb-rotated controls; turn signals on the left, the automatic transmission shifter to the right. An adjustable knob for a proposed "variable ratio steering" control was found in the wheel's hub.

Like those impractical side exhausts, that futuristic steering wheel was also left off of the Mako Shark's functional alter-ego, which was already in the works while the mockup was wowing New Yorkers in April 1965. When the 427-powered Mako was shown to the press on October 5, it had a typically round steering wheel. Cylindrical-shaped controls for the turn signals and the Turbo Hydra-Matic transmission were now found in familiar locations on either side of the steering column. In place of the side pipes was a conventional full-length exhaust system exiting through two highly stylized rectangular tips at the car's tail.

Gizmos and gimmicks, most of them electrical, abounded throughout the car. The six round taillights (three to a side) in back blinked in sequence, inner light to outer, in Thunderbird fashion, when the turn signals were activated. Working in concert with the front signals were cornering lights hidden behind four "gills" just ahead of each wheel. If the headlights were on when the turn signal was flicked, these gills opened up to let those lights show the way around corners. The driver was alerted to any power failure by a series of console-mounted indicators connected to each driving light by fiber-optic strands.

Headlights consisted of three quartz-iodide beams on a side hidden by long, thin "eyelids" that opened electrically. Though these lights were too low and too bright to be legal in the United States, no one ever stopped the show to make a citizen's arrest during the Mako Shark tour.

Electrical wonderment inside included a digital clock and two other digital readouts for both the fuel gauge and speedometer. Digital instruments are taken for granted today, but represented cutting-edge (and difficultly performed) techno-wizardry in 1965. Rocker switches abounded on the console and door panels as all conventional conveniences were electrically controlled: locks, side glass, and wiper/washers. Washer fluid was "piped" up the wiper arms to flood the Vee'ed windshield where it needed flooding the most—directly in front of the wiper blades. When not in use, those wiper arms hid themselves away beneath hinged cowl sections at the base of the windshield. Additional switches controlled the definitely unconventional rear window louvers, adjustable top-mounted headrests, and flip-up roof.

The electric motors that controlled those last three features were among 17 remote power units required to make all the Mako's toys work. These included a flush-mounted bumper bar in back that extended outward at the flick of one of those console switches. Another switch next to this one flipped the rear license plate around to hide it from view. Although it was claimed that this trick was added to allow the car's tail to appear less cluttered ("for unbroken styling lines," in press release words) on the auto show stage, another value became instantly apparent to street racers who understood the importance of anonymity while leaving the local constabulary in the dust. And wouldn't you know it, Bill Mitchell was one of Woodward Avenue's more famous drag kings.

One more electrical trick attracted a chuckle or two 35 years ago. But it was Mitchell who again got the last laugh. A switch next to the turn signal activator could raise a pair of spoilers as high as 4 inches above that duck-tailed lip in back. According to Chevrolet press releases, these aircraft-like "stability" flaps "increase the down-force or loading by the car's airstream." Skeptics weren't so sure.

"Their effectiveness must be open to debate," wrote *Car Life*'s Dennis Shattuck. "However, the 'stabilizers' make good conversation pieces." They have since made more than that. Many designers later followed Mitchell's lead and put automatically adjustable rear spoilers to work on some of the world's best sports cars. Look who's conversing now.

Shattuck was one of the Mako Shark II's most outspoken critics. Most magazines raved about the car, but not *Car Life*. According to Shattuck's January 1966 review, the Mako Shark II "amply illustrates the 'surface entertainment' idiom. [This] consists of a particular talent to take something that is basically good and clean and pure, then embellish upon it with emblems or textures or patterns which have no relationship with function, but appear to."

Road & Track's critics were much harsher. "The design of the body and the 'styling' of it are, as so often with GM cars, two separate concepts," began an August 1965 *R&T* review of the Mako Shark II mockup. "The basic lines are pleasing and exciting—squint your eyes and see. But styling gimmicks and details have been heaped upon it in such abundance that it's really difficult to see the lines. We suppose that this treatment is some kind of entertainment for the masses. Entertainment it is, in the same vein as comic books or pornography."

On a much more positive note, Shattuck did point out that turning heads was the Mako Shark's top priority. "Its coloration is attention-getting and the car no doubt will stir plenty of discussion, which is just what GM wants," he wrote. On the flipside, he still felt that less should have been more. "The overall shape and proportion is interesting and exciting—it's just that there are too many extraneous convolutions."

So much for form. As far as function was concerned, however, Shattuck was a bit more complimentary. "The car is nonetheless noteworthy," he wrote, "as it contains a variety of potentially available gadgets. In that regard, the Mako Shark II must be regarded as a rolling showcase for future options." Like any successful executive, Mitchell had already covered his ass, offering a disclaimer of sorts concerning that showcase. "Most of these features require further refinement and evaluation before being adopted on production models," he said. To that, Shattuck couldn't resist one last jab. "The Mako Shark II will continue to serve as a styling idea model, updated from time to time with various portions and contours and systems being plucked off it and manufactured on [other] production cars," he concluded. "Boy, just wait until they put those stabilizer flaps onto the Impala!"

Larry Shinoda later tried to put such slings and arrows into perspective. "There was certainly no shortage of reaction in the automobile media to some of the [Mako Shark's] 'added' features that Bill had requested even when some of it might have been just a little short-sighted," he told *Shark Quarterly* in 1997. "But that's the purpose of some of these cars. The public reaction has to be interpreted; you don't just take it at face value. People, by and large, tend to think 'right now' while we are supposed to think in the future. As I look back on the articles which have been written about the car 20 years later, I see a lot of retrospection. The authors now recognize the fact that some of the original criticisms were off-base; the core ideas have been realized."

Most of that criticism was lost beneath the praises heaped on the Mako Shark II during its world tour in 1966. After its press introduction, it was flown to France for an appearance at the Paris Automobile Salon on October 7, 1965. From there it went to London, Turin, Brussels, and Geneva before returning to America for the New York Auto Show in April 1966.

"It was an exceptionally beautiful car that had nothing to do with European nor, what is

more, with American style, but just with simple, pure style: neat, aerodynamic, and perfect," claimed *Styled Auto*'s staff. "It was a demonstration on how, in a field dominated by chromed, oversprung dinosaurs, an absolutely new and functional car can be made with great ingenuity and simplicity."

"It hasn't the functional beauty and purity of Pininfarina's Ferrari 275 Berlinetta, which anyone would be glad to be seen in," reported *Autocar*. "But let's give it full marks for showmanship and a taste of what is to come."

Once off the showcar circuit, the Mako Shark II paced a few races and also, like other Corvette showcars, served time as Bill Mitchell's personal driver. Then in 1969 it took on a new identity after it was restyled into the Manta Ray. Already measuring some 9 inches longer than a standard Sting Ray, the Mako Shark length grew even more after the Manta Ray conversion. Extra inches came by way of a restyled, stretched tail that took on a tapered look from a profile

perspective. The point of that tail was protected by a body-colored Endura bumper. And the louvered rear glass was replaced by a less practical (if that was possible) "sugar scoop" design that featured a radically scaled-down version of the tunneled rear window idea used on the XP-819. The Manta Ray's roofline too came together to a point like the Mako Shark.

Among other updates was a chin spoiler up front and a repaint that played down the shark shading. Side pipes were later added, as were small mirrors mounted up high on the windshield pillars. The biggest news, though, was the Manta Ray's new power source. In place of the iron-block 427 used by the Mako Shark came Chevrolet's all-aluminum ZL-1 427, an exotic, mean-and-nasty mill more befitting of an exotic, one-of-a-kind showcar.

Estimates put the price tag for the original 427-powered Mako Shark II at as much as $2.5 million. Reportedly that price may have even hit $3 million by the time the ZL-1 Manta Ray

In place of the Mako Shark II's rear louvers, the Manta Ray was fitted with a miniscule "sugar scoop" rear window layout. Side exhausts also returned. *Courtesy Automobile Quarterly*

Power for the
Manta Ray was
updated with the
addition of an
aluminum ZL-1
427. *Courtesy
Automobile
Quarterly*

transformation was complete. Was it worth it? What do you think? Publicity may have never come GM's way at a better price per pound. And so much of what made the Mako Shark a show-stopper did find its way into the production Corvette in 1968. Whether that was good or bad can be debated, and was. But one plain fact can't be denied: Corvette popularity reached record heights nearly every year during the third-generation run.

Much work still remained ahead in 1966 if Chevrolet was to make the jump from Mako Shark II to a regular-production Corvette in time for the originally planned 1967 introduction. Design teams were still eating up valuable work weeks toying with Duntov's midengined ideal. Yet another such proposal, mocked up by Mitchell's stylists, appeared in March 1966. This one wore a body with fully enclosed rear wheels and no rear window—rear-view vision was provided by a telescope of all things.

Other more practical midengine experimental models soon followed, but the idea of the perfectly balanced, lightweight Corvette remained a dream. In 1957, planners had run up against retooling costs for the Q-Corvette's original rear-transmission design. That inhibiting reality remained plainly clear 10 years later. The steep price for an all-new

transmission/transaxle layout alone was enough to keep the midengine Corvette on the shelf. Despite continued wishful thinking in the press, the next best Vette yet would remain of conventional, front-engined design.

That design was mocked up late in 1964 in Shinoda's secret studio. Compared to the Mako Shark II, this second theme was fashioned more conservatively with practical production in mind. But it still mirrored the basic Mako profile to come. It had a similar tapered roofline and a one-piece top that, in this case, could be completely removed from the car. That Targa-top idea was "borrowed" from the European sports car scene, a move Mitchell wasn't ashamed of in the least. As he told *Collectible Automobile* in 1984, "I wasn't above stealing things from European cars. Not American cars—there was nothing over here to steal."

While Shinoda was busy finishing his model, Henry Haga's team was completing a competing mockup in the regular production studio. Both were then viewed by Mitchell. Haga's car featured soft, rounded lines. "It had a little bit of a flying saucer look to it," said Shinoda later in a *Collectible Automobile* interview. "And Mitchell hated it. He said, 'have you ever seen such a fat pig?' Then he kicked it, and almost the whole back end fell off!"

Mitchell chose Shinoda's theme and passed it on to Haga's studio for its transformation into reality. One of the first changes made was to trade that "boat-tail" roof for a more practical, more pleasing design also borrowed from Europe—in this case, from the Porsche 904. Vertical rear glass was sandwiched between two parallel "flying buttress" C-pillars, a layout that recreated the "tunneled" window style used on XP-819.

The Targa-top idea, also used on XP-819, initially carried over into Haga's studio. And it remained in place atop prototypes until the last minute. With no fixed roof structure in place to help stiffen the platform, the Targa-top machines flexed too much, allowing their windshield frames to twist in relation to the rear roofline "arch." This unwanted torsional movement made the top creak, and it also compromised the car's weather-sealing capabilities. Duntov's crew couldn't solve this problem within established parameters so they had no choice but to add a central reinforcing strut to join the windshield header to that arch. This in turn meant the one-piece roof had to be separated into two sections.

Fixing the roof, however, was the least of Duntov's worries. By then, he had already asked Pete Estes for a deadline extension and gotten his extra year. As mentioned, this time was needed to address various gremlins hiding within that oversexed body. Shinoda's shape was too curvaceous, too bulging. Outward visibility was severely hindered by those tall fender tops; that low, flying-buttress roof; and the big ducktail in back. The slinky shell was also too close to the ground in front where that sharp-edged beak limited the amount of cooling air able to reach the engine. And let's not forget aerodynamics.

An engineering test vehicle was touring GM's Milford Proving Grounds as early as the fall of 1965. A new 1965 Corvette was also run around the track to serve as a measuring stick. Duntov's "bad airplane" tended to lift at both ends at high speeds. At 120 miles per hour, the 1965 Sting Ray's nose rose 2.25 inches, the rear 1/2 inch. In comparison, Engineering's test car hunkered down in back at speed thanks to that large rear spoiler. At 120 miles per hour, its tail dropped 1/4 inch. This depression in turn helped raise the nose, a task the car could already handle well enough on its own. Lift at 120 miles per hour measured 3.75 inches. That first test car might have easily handled regular nonstop service from Dayton to Chicago with scheduled takeoffs every hour on the hour.

All that lift not only made high-speed travel an unstable, turbulent, if not frightening experience, it also typically increased drag. And as all aeronautical engineers know, more drag means more propulsion is needed to reach high speeds. For the record, the 1965 Corvette had to deliver 155 horsepower to the road to attain 120 miles per hour. Engineering's test machine initially required 210 horses to hit the same speed.

Bringing things back down to earth was first achieved by venting the front fenders, a trick first tried on Jim Hall's Chaparral race cars. These vents allowed trapped airflow up front a quicker exit, thus reducing nose lift at the top end. Opening up the fenders brought the prototype's lift down close to stock 1965 Sting Ray levels. At the same time, the modification meant only 175 horsepower was needed to move the car up to 120 miles per hour. Adding a chin spoiler up front—again ala the Chaparral—reduced that power requirement even further to a mere 105 horses. That spoiler also sliced lift to a measly 5/8 of an inch.

Slicing and dicing didn't end there, and it was all the additionally required bodywork that finally convinced everyone involved to push the planned delivery date back from 1967 to 1968. Haga's stylists, joined by Larry Shinoda, took the body back into the studio to address Duntov's other complaints. They cut down those front fender tops to allow the driver a safer look ahead. The rear quarters and roofline were also modified to improve rearward visibility. Downsizing the rear spoiler into a molded-in lip further enhanced the view.

Engine cooling was aided by a reshaped nose that allowed the radiator a more prominent location up front. An "air-dam" lip that ran beneath the car and up around the front wheel openings was also added to better direct cool air toward that radiator. Finally, those fender vents were enlarged to help let hot air escape more easily from beneath the hood. The last two modifications also helped decrease high-speed lift too.

When everything was said and done, the next great Corvette was finally ready for customer deliveries in the fall of 1967. Or was it?

Chapter 2

SEE THREE
Introducing the Latest, Greatest Corvette

Zora Duntov already had enough to deal with in 1967. He became seriously ill that spring and was hospitalized for most of May and June. On top of that, he also was forced to face the reality that the Corvette was no longer his baby. Chevrolet's supposedly wise decision-makers had placed the teenaged two-seater into a foster home late in the C3's birthing process. Even though no one else at GM understood the Corvette as well as Zora, management restructuring at Chevrolet still took America's only sports car out of his capable hands and placed it under the care of the same engineers responsible for the division's full-sized passenger automobiles.

So much for autonomy—for both man and machine. When Duntov emerged from the hospital he found he was now a consultant to the chief engineer's office and the Corvette was just another face in the crowd at Chevrolet Engineering. His authority was all but gone. But the third-generation Corvette's teething problems weren't. Normally all major pains are eased by this late stage in a new-model development process. Not so with the 1968 Corvette.

Before he entered the hospital, Duntov requested that Chevrolet chief engineer Jim Premo personally address one particular hot spot. Sizzling, sexy looks weren't the Shark body's only claim to fame. Excessive heat beneath the hood remained an inherent irritation throughout the third-generation Corvette's long roll into production. Premo undoubtedly recognized the need to soothe this flare-up, but he was reassigned by GM's front office before he could address the problem. His replacement at Chevy Engineering, Alex Mair, apparently concerned himself more with the entire waiting room full of patients instead of one seemingly minor (from his perspective) toothache. Remember, Mair's job was to oversee all of Chevrolet's passenger-car engineering, and the Corvette was now simply one of many Chevrolet products in need of attention. Not special attention, mind you, just attention. Nothing more, nothing less.

So it was that Chevrolet Engineering's restructured pecking order allowed the 1968 Corvette's inherent hot temper to simmer almost unchecked until Duntov returned to work early in July 1967. His first assignment as consultant was to prep the 1968 prototype for its long-awaited press preview, then less than a month away. But all he needed was one tour in the blue big-block coupe then being readied for journalists' scrutiny to recognize that the car would never keep its cool under the magnifying glass. Big-block Corvettes had always run hot, and this particular prototype was no exception. In truth, it was even more so due to that fact that all that cast iron was stuffed into stuffier confines. Not enough outside air could find its way into the radiator to help the coolant flowing within do its job.

Duntov's quick-fix saved the day. He opened up two oblong vents beneath the car's low-slung nose just ahead of the chin spoiler, then enlarged that spoiler to help increase the pressure forcing the airflow up into those openings. From there, the rush of air could only flow

Although it's wearing "Stingray" badges on its flanks, this LeMans Blue coupe is a 1968 model—no Corvettes that year were identified with the familiar script. Perhaps the car's late sales date—midway in August 1968—helps explain the addition. This Corvette perhaps was the last L-89 version built for 1968.

The L-89 option added lightweight aluminum heads to the 435-horsepower, L-71 427 big-block. Only 624 L-89 Corvettes were built for 1968.

The bare fenders on this Silverstone Silver coupe quickly give away its identity as a 1968 Corvette. Stingray badging appeared in 1969. Red-stripe F70x15 tires, RPO PT6, were a $31.30 option in 1968.

through the radiator as all gaps to either side were closed up. Presto. The big-block prototype ran all day long in 85-degree heat at the Milford Proving Ground during the press introduction, and the temperature gauge stayed within established parameters.

The last major pain relieved? Not exactly.

Immediately ahead for Duntov and his stepchild was one more serious headache. Chevrolet's reorganized plan to build the third-generation Corvette "by committee" created more problems than it supposedly cured. Conventional mass-production tactics worked for passenger cars like Chevelles and Novas, but not for the somewhat-finicky, fiberglass-bodied performance machine that Zora had always hoped would someday challenge the world's best sports cars. It didn't take long for nearly everyone with eyes outside GM to quickly notice how poorly the next great Corvette was being raised in its new home.

After introducing the 1968 prototype to the American press in Michigan, Duntov's next "special consultant" task involved taking another big-block coupe overseas to test European waters in the fall of 1967. Zora's good friend, Belgian journalist Paul Frere, gave the car's performance high marks in his *Motor* review. On the other hand, he also mentioned the body's various rattles and

Four 427 big-blocks were offered in 1968, counting the race-only L-88. Two engines, the 400-horsepower L-68 and 435-horsepower L-71, featured triple carburetors. The L-36 427, shown here, was fed by one four-barrel and produced 390 horsepower. L-36 Corvette production in 1968 was 7,717.

noises. It seemed that anyone with ears also took note.

Back in America, *Car and Driver* editor Steve Smith had both ears and eyes. He also had a sharp pen. In his December 1967 editorial Smith declared the 1968 Corvette he drove was "unfit for a road test." "With less than 2,000 miles on it, the Corvette was falling apart," he wrote. Hot performance couldn't turn his head. Instead he was far more concerned with "the car's shocking lack of quality control."

"Sometimes the pieces chafed against each other, sometimes they left wide gaps, sometimes they were just plain crooked," continued Smith about mismatched body panels. "In the rain, water leaked through a gap in the bolt-on hard-top and dripped on our left shoulders like the Chinese water torture. The surface of the fiber-glass was as wavy as a home-built layup. The car rattled and shook on mildly bumpy roads."

We can only wonder what Steve really thought.

As for Corvette customers, they were no strangers to imperfections in the molded shell. Body finish quality had fluctuated considerably during the original Sting Ray's five-year run. But it had never been this bad. And overall fit, as Smith explained, was now downright terrible. *Car and Driver*'s complaints would be echoed again and again by countless buyers who had the

misfortune of helping Chevrolet iron out the C3's bugs. To this day, the 1968 model still stands, in many opinions, as the most poorly constructed Corvette of all time. And those fit and finish maladies didn't go away overnight.

Chevrolet's immediate response to this quality-control problem was to right the wrong made midway in 1967. While customer complaints might have eventually inspired the same result, it was Steve Smith's caustic *C/D* column that probably did the most to help reunite the main man and his baby. In 1968, the Corvette program was restored to its rightful place as an exclusive engineering entity. And Zora Arkus-Duntov was finally promoted to the official position he had so long deserved—Corvette chief engineer. From then on, Duntov had the final say concerning essentially every facet of Corvette development and production.

One of the few cases (as well as the most significant) where Zora found himself shouted down in the chief engineer's seat involved the ongoing myth of the mid-engine Corvette. As early as 1965, witnesses were beginning to wonder if the next new two-seater would indeed appear with its engine mounted amidships, this after various scale models featuring this layout were constructed for developmental consideration.

Two years later, Frank Winchell put Larry Nies to work on the attractive XP-880. This

Save for some reworked suspension geometry in back, which in turn required some additional crimping of the exhaust pipes (notice the flattened tube just below the driveshaft), the Shark's chassis carried over from 1967. The triangle-shaped air cleaner on this big-block signifies the presence of the tri-carb 427. *Chevrolet Motor Division*

model looked a lot like their failed XP-819 Corvette with its rear-mounted small-block but actually relied on a Mk IV big-block V-8 bolted in between the driver and rear wheels. Not to be outdone, in 1968 Duntov's engineers began creating their own midengine prototype, the sensational XP-882. These experimental Corvettes were then followed in 1971 by the equally sensational XP-895. Two other more radical midengine machines, fitted with Wankel rotary engines instead of V-8s, appeared in 1973, leading more than one major magazine to announce the arrival of the next new Corvette.

Both *Road & Track* and *Car and Driver* had already made a habit of printing such wishful predictions, and little wonder. Staff opinions from both sources in the 1960s continually favored the exotic European sports car ideal, regardless of price. In their minds not only was the Corvette too conventional and way too heavy to compete with its much more expensive foreign rivals, it was also too blatantly American. "For those who like their cars big, flashy and full of blinking lights and trap doors, it's a winner," claimed an *R&T* review of the 1968 Corvette. On the other hand, "the connoisseur who values finesse, efficiency and the latest chassis design will have to look, unfortunately, to Europe."

By the time *Car and Driver*'s curbside critics did finally get around to road-testing a better-built third-generation Corvette (in their May 1968 issue), they called it "a brilliant car with all of the virtues and all of the vices of American technology. On balance, it's an almost irresistible temptation to buy American." That backhanded compliment, however, was followed a year later by a far less flattering line: "The Corvette's excellent engineering tends to be obscured by some rather garish styling gimmicks that make the uninitiated wonder if the car is a fake—a lurid, bulging, silicone-filled, automotive Playboy Bunny."

"This confusing identity is the result of a confrontation on the part of Zora Arkus-Duntov, who is well and truly the patron saint of all Corvettes, and the Chevrolet styling department," continued that September 1969 *C/D* report. "Duntov's primary aim in his professional life is to make the Corvette the finest sports car in the world. The styling department views his car as a unique opportunity to fool around with the swoopy shapes and flashing lights that somehow to them mean 'sport.' It is within this minor tempest that the Corvette encounters trouble: Duntov on the one hand viewing his automobile as a purposeful, well-balanced sports car, while his rivals see it as a Flash Gordon Thunderbird for the Hugh Hefner school of mass-cult glamour."

Road & Track's staffers were also disappointed in Chevrolet's apparent decision to emphasize flash over innovation. "Rumors came and went about an exciting, advanced new Corvette that would package the engine in the 'midship' position now almost universal in racing machinery and feature new, more efficient body-chassis construction," read *R&T*'s January 1968 road test. "But, alas, all the available money was spent on new styling."

A year later, *Car and Driver* went one step further concerning the prospects of an advanced new Corvette. "The present Corvette will doubtlessly be the last front-engine model," predicted *C/D*. "It remains uncertain if the new rear-engine [sic] version will be introduced in 1971 or 1972. Although a number of prototypes have been tested, a certain amount of turmoil exists within Chevrolet as to exactly what form the new car will take. The present general manager, John DeLorean, is as much an automotive purist as ever reached the top ranks at General Motors, and it is known that he is unhappy with the present Corvette. Rumors from deep inside the company indicate that De-Lorean has pronounced that the mid-engine version must be a functional sports/GT car weighing in the neighborhood of 2,600 lbs. and containing an engine of about 400 ci. This places a giant challenge before Duntov and his engineers. [Whether] this can be accomplished with a fiberglass or steel body remains to be seen, but it can be assumed that DeLorean, an engineer himself, will drive hard to make the new Corvette lean and tough. If he succeeds, it could mean goodbye to the [existing] jet-plane gimmickry. And for that we'd all be thankful."

Even more predictions followed, most prominently from *Road & Track*. In 1970, an *R&T* report claimed a midengine Corvette definitely was on the way for 1972; in 1971 yet another feature gave us the "first look" at the "1973 mid-engine Corvette." As late as 1977, *Road & Track*'s ever-optimistic editors were still predicting the arrival of an all-new midmotored Corvette, this time for 1980.

Duntov's dreams for the perfectly balanced, lighweight Corvette, however, had already been dashed well before that last *Road & Track* prophecy hit the stands. Fantasies would be more like it. Zora, Shinoda, Winchell—they all could've built midengine prototypes until the cows made it home and they still wouldn't have affected reality. GM's executive opinion of the plan was plain and simple: Why fix something that wasn't broken? Corvette sales set new records in 1968 and 1969, then started over in 1970 on a steady rise that didn't peak until 1977. Chevrolet held a captive audience for its fiberglass two-seater (with its front-mounted engine) during the 1970s and everyone from DeLorean on up knew it. Even so, corporate execs still allowed Duntov to dream on almost right up to his retirement in early 1975.

When GM squelched the midengine Corvette proposal it resulted in one of the greatest disappointments Zora encountered during his 21 years working with America's only sports car. "Until 1970, 90 percent of what I intended to do, I accomplished," said the Corvette's first chief engineer in a 1980 *Auto-Week* interview. "In 1972, a mid-ship car was touch and go. It was all designed." But it still wasn't to be.

That downer still lay well ahead for Duntov while he was working overtime to rid the new third-generation Corvette of those unwelcomed gremlins. Yet even with its obvious

Body drop time for a 1968 coupe at the St. Louis assembly plant. The powertrain is the base 300-horsepower 327 backed by the optional Turbo Hydra-Matic automatic transmission.

Restyled fender
louvers were
added in 1970,
as were flared
wheel openings
to help resist
rock chip damage
to the body.

quality-control problems and conventionally located engine, the 1968 Corvette by no means disappointed red-white-and-blue-blooded buyers. By the time the dust cleared, 28,566 of them had stormed Chevrolet dealerships for their own private piece of the ongoing Corvette legacy.

Not all among the automotive press were inclined to sling arrows, either. Far more chauvinistic than *R&T* or *C/D*, *Car Life* couldn't brag enough about the hot, new, built-in-the-U.S.A performance car it described as "the excitement generator." "This 1968 sport coupe is endowed with smooth ferocity," continued *Car Life*'s first review of the latest Corvette. "Longer, lower, wider and sleeker, the new fiberglass envelope should cause a stampede among American sports car purchasers."

Most buyers with a need for speed in this country in 1968 couldn't have cared less about foregoing any possible Continental considerations. These love-it-or-leave-it performance car partisans also didn't need some Euro-phile magazine editor telling them what they should or shouldn't like. They adored big American cars with big American horsepower. Many of them also had nothing against Playboy Bunnies or

Flash Gordon, either. And they certainly had no complaints about the Corvette's new look, which titillated them like no Corvette before with its seething, American-style sensuality.

From its low, pointed nose to its flared tail, the 1968 Corvette quickened pulses every bit as easily as the Mako Shark II had done three years before. Those sleek looks also did a decent job of cheating the wind, although most critics still pointed out that much of the car's aerodynamic performance remained a mirage. Less so, however, than in 1967. Test figures for drag and high-speed lift were, according to *Sports Car Graphic*'s Paul Van Valkenburgh in 1970, "very respectable considering that the shape was dictated by GM Styling, and Chevrolet engineers had to sweat acid trying to keep the nose on the ground at speeds over 150."

Although the C3 Corvette gained some high-speed abilities compared to its midyear forerunners, it lost a little ground on the scales, where it weighed in at nearly 3,300 pounds, roughly 150 more than the Sting Ray. It was also 7 inches longer overall at 182.5 clicks. At 69 inches, width was two-tenths less than in 1967, while height dropped from 49.6 inches to 47.8.

The L-46 small-block, a 350-ci derivative of the 327-ci L-79 V-8, was last offered in 1970. A slightly tamed version of the LT-1 350 with hydraulic lifters instead of mechanical tappets, the L-46, like the L-79, was rated at 350 horsepower. L-46 Corvette production in 1970 was 4,910.

Those last two measurements, working in concert with the radically increased "tumble-home" of the rounded Shark bodysides, translated into a considerable reduction in interior space, demonstrating once more just how much Mitchell's styling dictators controlled the car's functions.

That sexy, claustrophobic form wasn't the only thing to carry over from the auto show stage into production. While the T-top roof superceded the Mako Shark II's one-piece targa top, the production Corvette did share various other design features with its showcar forerunner, not the least of which was its fiber-optic warning light system and its hidden windshield wipers. The latter rested below a vacuum-operated panel that popped open on demand whenever the forecast called for rain. Sleet or snow sometimes represented another situation entirely, although Chevrolet designers claimed that the wipers' lid, as well as the car's vacuum-activated pop-up headlights, could crack their way through 3/8-inch-thick ice. But who would dare subject their 'glass-bodied baby to such climatic calamity, right?

Like the Mako Shark, the 1968 Corvette also arrived without vent windows. Letting the good air in, bad air out was now the job of Chevrolet's new "Astro" ventilation system, which routed fresh breezes in through the cowl,

The ever-popular tilt-telescopic steering column, RPO N37, cost $84 in 1970. N37 sales that year totaled 5,803. This particular L-46 coupe is also equipped with air conditioning, something LT-1 drivers couldn't enjoy until late in 1972.

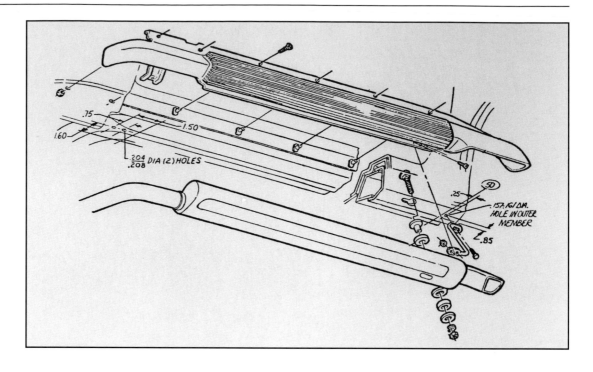

around interior airspace, and out through grilles located in the rear deck right behind the back window. Convertibles used this ductwork too. Coupe owners in need of a little more wind, along with some extra tanning time, of course could've removed their T-tops. That rear glass detached as well for maximum mussing of the hair, however many follicles remained.

Like the midyear Sting Rays it replaced, the C3 Corvette's first bodystyle rolled on in essentially identical fashion through five model runs. The basic profile, the T-tops, the coupe's removable window—all these readily identifiable features continued unchanged up through 1972. Same for the wheels. Although they were widened from 7 inches to 8 beginning in 1969, those standard 15-inch Rally rims retained an identical style each year, as did the optional full wheelcovers.

While the annual list of minor revamps, inside and out, is a long one, most casual witnesses at a glance still find it difficult to differentiate the Corvettes built from 1968 to 1972. Quick, easy, one-guess giveaways included the optional side-mount exhausts, which were only offered in 1969, and the separate rectangular backup lights, which were of 1968 only. Another less noticeable option, RPO TJ2, added bright trim to the Corvette's fender louvers in 1969 only. The 1968 door handles and dash-mounted ignition switch were also unique. In 1969, the ignition went to

the steering column, the pushbutton door releases were deleted, and the backup lights were moved up into the center of the inner pair of taillights. The taillight lenses themselves were later revised slightly in late 1971.

Probably the most obvious clue concerning the 1968 Corvette's true identity involved badging. The Sting Ray name was nowhere to be found on that swoopy shape. Perhaps Chevrolet officials finally opened a dictionary and chose to erase their error. Most spelling compilations describe yet another of Bill Mitchell's favorite sea creatures using one word, as Mitchell himself had done in 1959 for his Shinoda-bodied racer. Whatever the case, when the second edition C3 appeared in 1969 a correctly spelled "Stingray" script was placed on each flank directly above those fender "gills."

Less specific were the round exhaust tips and bezels used in both 1968 and 1969. These units became rectangles on 1970–72 Corvettes. Corvettes in 1968 and 1969 also featured their own style of vertical fender vent; the 1970–72 group received a revised vent that was topped by a bright crosshatch grille. Along with that, 1970–72 Corvettes were fitted with larger side marker lights and rectangular turn signals up front. The 1968–69 models used round turn signal lamps and smaller side markers. The Shark shell in 1970 was also mildly modified with flares around the wheel openings.

Among the various far less obvious changes made during the 1968–72 run was the deletion of the transistorized ignition and optic-fiber warning light system after 1971. In exchange for the latter, Corvette drivers in 1972 received a horn-honking burglar alarm system as standard equipment. The alarm system was previously an option, RPO UA6, for 1968–71 Corvettes.

Nearly all engineering features beneath the Shark's skin were familiar to any Sting Ray owner who had crawled under a midyear model for a peek. Indeed, all the money had been spent on new styling. Holding up the 1968 Corvette's dirty side was basically the same chassis introduced in 1963, it with the 98-inch wheelbase and independent rear suspension. That's not to say that Duntov didn't have a trick or two up his sleeve.

Yet another inherent problem he addressed in 1968 was the Sting Ray's habit of pitching its nose up whenever the go-pedal was mashed to the floor. Once the nose raised, front wheel geometry went wildly out of whack, meaning the car tended to wander at a time when precise control was preferred more than ever. To help correct this malady, spring rates were stiffened and the rear roll center was dropped from 7.56 inches above the ground to 4.71 inches by lowering the inner pivot points of the lateral suspension arms. Then, to compensate for the

increased understeer "dialed in" by these changes, those widened 7-inch Rally wheels were added to allow the use of fatter F70x15 tires. More rubber on the ground meant more resistance to lateral g-forces. Maximum lateral acceleration measured 0.84g for the 1968 Corvette, compared to 0.74 for the Sting Ray. Those wider wheels and tires also meant an increase in track: from 56.8 inches to 58.7 in front and from 57.6 to 59.4 in back.

Did these modifications do the trick? Even *Road & Track*'s ever-critical critics were impressed. "No question about it, the Corvette is one of the best-handling front-engine production cars in the world," claimed a 1969 *R&T* road test.

Initially the C3's standard drivetrain was a complete midyear carryover. Included in the 1968 Corvette's base price ($4,663 for a coupe, $4,320 for a convertible) was the same tried-and-true 300-horse 327 small-block and three-speed manual gearbox installed as standard equipment since 1966. The 327/300 V-8 actually first appeared as an option four years earlier.

Base engine specs then began to grow along with those prices in 1969. A standard 1969 coupe cost $4,781; a convertible, $4,438. Included in both of those deals was a bigger small-block V-8, the 350. Chevrolet engineers had created the 350 in 1967 by stretching the 327's 3.25-inch stroke to 3.48 inches. Bore remained

A removable hardtop, RPO C07, was a $273 option for a Corvette convertible in 1970. Adding vinyl covering (RPO C08) to that roof cost another $63. C07 sales totaled 2,556 that year. Only 832 vinyl roofs were sold.

at 4.00 inches. In the 1969 Corvette's case, almost all other numbers also carried over from the 327 to the 350. Compression remained at 10.25:1 and maximum output was still 300 horsepower at 5,000 rpm. Maximum torque, however, went from 360 ft-lb at 3,400 rpm up to 380 at the same revolutions.

Advertised power levels for the base 350 repeated themselves in 1970 (at slightly lower rpm peaks), then began to drop for the first time in Corvette history in 1971. The reason for the decrease was a compression cut (to 8.5:1) made as part of GM's response to a federal government crackdown on engine emissions. While an even tighter environmentally conscious stranglehold on horsepower lay ahead, advertised outputs for all of GM's engines plummeted further in 1972 when gross ratings were traded for SAE net figures. The 1972 Corvette's standard 350 was listed at a paltry 200 net horsepower.

As for optional engines, the 1968 list was identical to 1967's right down to the prices. At the bottom was the L-79 327, rated at 350 horses. While the L-79's hydraulic lifters helped keep it on the tame side, its 11:1 compression promised wilder times. The price for RPO L-79 was $105.35.

Next came the 427 big-blocks, or "rat motors" as Chevy freaks like to call the division's big-cube Mk IV V-8s. The 390-horsepower L-36 cost $200.15; the 400-horsepower L-68, $305.50; and the thunderous 435-horsepower L-71,

$437.10. Topping everything off was the race-ready L-88 427 and the L-89 aluminum head package for the L-71. Prices were $805.75 for the L-89/L-71 and $947.90 for the legendary L-88 with its token 430-horse rating. Production was 7,717 for the L-36, 1,932 for the L-68, 2,898 for the L-71, 624 for the L-89, and 80 for the L-88.

All these 427s—save for the L-88—were fitted with new "low-rise" intake manifolds designed to allow the carburetor (or carburetors) ample clearance beneath the third-generation Corvette's low, low hood. Efficient intake flow (and thus power) was preserved by "sinking" the manifold's underside into the big-block's lifter valley. L-88's didn't require this modification because the scoop on their cool-air hoods supplied the needed carb clearance.

The L-36 and L-68 427s were essentially identical, save for one major adjustment. Both produced their maximum 460 ft-lb of torque at 3,600 rpm. Both also compressed their fuel/air mixture at a 10.25:1 ratio. But while the L-36 relied on a single Rochester Quadrajet four-barrel to shoot the juice, the L-68 sucked down the high-test through the trick triple-carb induction setup introduced for the 1967 Sting Ray. "Three 2-bbl Holley carburetors are used," explained Car and Driver's May 1968 L-68 test, "with the one in the middle providing for normal operation while the end ones, with their vacuum operated throttles, are useful for setting land speed records and snaffling traffic tickets."

Like the L-68, the L-71 too was fed by three Holleys. But it was an entirely different beast. Head-cracking compression was 11.0:1. Four-bolt main bearing caps held the bottom end together. A lumpier cam hammered away at mechanical tappets instead of hydraulic lifters. The K66 transistorized ignition was a required option, as was the M21 close-ratio four-speed transmission.

Those solid lifters allowed the big, hairy L-71 to wind out longer than the L-68 before the muscle fell off. The L-71's 460 pounds of torque arrived at 4,000 rpm. Its 435 hell-bent-for-leather horses showed up at 5,800 revs. As in 1967, the L-71 Corvette in 1968 remained one of America's quickest street machines—road tests produced quarter-mile times in the low (make that very low) 13-second bracket. For more on the even stronger L-88s of 1968 and 1969, see chapter 3.

Changes to the extra-cost engine lineup in 1969 included two new codes. RPO L-46 was added to the small-block ranks to mark the popular 350-horse V-8's graduation from 327 ci to 350. Actually, L-46 replaced L-79. The other code, RPO ZL-1, represented an entirely new breed of 427 V-8, this one with an aluminum block to go along with the L-88's aluminum heads. Again, check out chapter 3 for the tale of the two known factory-installed ZL-1 Corvettes.

All the other optional 427s—they with their cast-iron blocks—rolled over from 1968. Production in 1969 was 10,531 for the L-36, 2,072 for the L-68, 2,772 for the L-71, 390 for the L-89, and 116 for the L-88.

Additional optional upgrades included the introduction of the Corvette's biggest big-block, the 454, in 1970. This monster mill, like the 350 small-block, represented another "stroke of genius" by Chevy engineers. Knowing full well that there was then no substitute for cubic inches, they simply stroked the 427 (from 3.76 inches to 4.00) to add another 27 cubes. The 4.25-inch bore remained constant, as did compression and horsepower. Like the L-36 427 of 1969, the LS-5 454 of 1970 squeezed fuel/air molecules at a 10.25:1 ratio to help churn out 390 maximum horses at 5,400 rpm. Torque output, on the other hand, was a whopping 500 ft-lb, 40 more than the L-36.

While it could melt a Wide Oval with the best of 'em and gulp a gallon of ethyl quicker than you could pump her in, the high-compression 454 in 1970 still could've been considered quite user friendly, thanks in part to its hydraulic cam. "It is by far the most tractable big-engine Corvette unit we've tried," claimed a *Road & Track* road test of the 1970 LS-5 Corvette. At $289.65, RPO LS-5 also wasn't all that hard on the wallet, especially compared to its new little brother, the LT-1 small-block, which cost that plus another $150 or so in spare change in 1970.

Whether or not 440 bucks (or the $480 charged in 1971) was too much to pay for a small-block V-8 depended upon how much a Corvette driver liked playing David to a big-block musclecar owner's Goliath. Rated at 370 horsepower, the first LT-1 solid-lifter 350 could easily slug it out with engines that displaced 100 more cubes, and did so with a vengeance up through 1972. In Corvette terms, the much lighter LT-1 offered customers better handling and similar acceleration in comparison to the nose-heavy big-block models. "As you would expect, the personalities of the LS-5 and the LT-1 are worlds apart," explained a *Car and Driver* review of the Corvette's many different moods. "In performance however, they are neck and neck." To read all about the LT-1, see chapter 4.

The LS-5 gentle giant became even easier to get along with in 1971 after compression was cut to 8.5:1. Advertised output, in turn, dropped to 365 horsepower. Maximum torque slipped to 465 ft-lb at 3,200 rpm. Yet performance still remained high. Rest to 60 miles per hour required only 5.7 seconds according to a *Car and Driver* test, which also reported that the quarter-mile rolled by in 14.1 clicks.

If that wasn't hot enough for you, there was yet another big-block option. The LS-6 454, which first appeared with its 450 horses beneath Chevelle SS hoods in 1970, made its way onto the Corvette options list in 1971 in place of the stillborn 460-horsepower LS-7 promised the year before. Even with compression sliced down from 11.25:1 (in Chevelle trim) to 9:1, the Corvette's LS-6 still produced 425 horsepower, more than enough muscle to propel a fiberglass body into the 13-second quarter-mile bracket. Once more run, don't walk, to chapter 3 to catch up with the rare, rarin'-to-go LS-6 Corvette and the mysterious LS-7 454.

Unfortunately the LS-6 was a one-hit wonder, and understandably so considering how

Coupes outnumbered convertibles by nearly a 2-to-1 margin in 1971, signaling a downward slide that would lead to the topless Corvette's demise four years later.

The fiber-optic light monitoring system, introduced in 1968, was used for the last time in 1971. Those monitor lights appear just below the AM/FM radio on this 1971 convertible.

quickly gas-guzzling, air-fouling big-block V-8s lost face with both the public and GM execs in the early 1970s. Even if Washington in the late-1960s hadn't targeted the internal combustion engine as the main culprit behind this country's air pollution problem, those heavy, high-priced eight-cylinder indulgences would've still run afoul of changing trends and attitudes once gasoline began turning into gold around 1973.

By then the changing trend at Chevrolet involved numbers crunching. Not pricing or production, mind you, those figures continued to rise. But with Corvette demand higher than ever, GM decision-makers began to question the reasons to stock the shelves with so many costly engines. Cylinder heads then started to roll. Counting the L-89 option and the exotic ZL-1, there were seven engine options offered along with the standard 350 in 1969. The Corvette's engine lineup shrank to five early in 1970, then four after the uncivilized LS-7 was cancelled before it could escape into the wild. Gone were all those extra carburetors and aluminum heads that had helped make the 427 the stuff of Corvette owners' dreams.

It was four again in 1971 as a new aluminum-head big-block, the LS-6, debuted while a veteran small-block, the 350-horse

350, retired. Born in 1965 as the L-79 327, the 350-horsepower small-block quickly formed a healthy following. L-79 production that first year was 4,716, followed by 7,591 in 1966 and 6,375 in 1967. Sales jumped to 9,440 in 1968, then reached 12,846 for the 350-cube L-46 rendition in 1969. "Only" 4,910 L-46 Corvettes were sold during 1970's shortened production run.

What was so great about the L-79/L-46? Why did Chevrolet officials drop it like a hot potato after 1970? Why did chief engineer Duntov let them? Last thing first. Zora basically didn't have a choice. Or did he? GM penny-pinchers in 1971 demanded that an engine be dropped from the Corvette lineup, and it was either the LT-1 or the L-46. Duntov campaigned for the former to help keep his baby ahead of the performance pack, though he wasn't happy at all about seeing the popular 350-horse 350 ride away into the sunset.

"He has harsh words for the 'bean counters' who occasionally eliminate a worthwhile option or feature," explained a June 1971 *Car and Driver* report. "The L-46 for example. Until this year you could buy a 350-ci. 350-horsepower engine with a hydraulic camshaft that had very nearly the performance of the LT-1

but was also compatible with air conditioning. And you could buy it for about $150 compared to $483 for the LT-1. 'Redundant,' decided the bean counters and axed it off the list. Duntov thinks otherwise."

GM decision-makers, though, couldn't have cared less about what Zora thought in this case. At the time, *performance* had become a dirty word at GM, and an anti-Corvette groundswell among corporate killjoys who questioned the money spent on a narrow-niche product like the fiberglass two-seater was just developing. Not even record sales could convince this faction that the return was worth the investment. The LS-7 big-block never saw the light of day in 1970 due to GM's overnight change in attitude concerning the sale of unbridled horsepower. And when execs raised the axe again in 1971, not even the L-46's successful record could save its neck.

Like its L-79 predecessor, the L-46 thrived in its day simply because it was such a great deal. It represented a Corvette customer's best buy as far as horsepower-per-dollar was concerned. It was also far easier to live with than the solid-lifter LT-1, and not just because its driver could stay cooler behind the wheel. That hydraulic cam meant no maintenance

hassles and less underhood noise. The LT-1 package also included a stiffer suspension that further compromised the third-generation Corvette's already shaky ride comfort. Ask most drivers who opted for the L-46 in 1970 instead of the LT-1, and they'll tell you the 20-horse trade-off was offset by improved seat-of-the-pants responses and the absence of those pesky solid lifters.

A year after the L-46 was cut, the LS-6 big-block too went as quickly as it had come, leaving Corvette buyers with only three net-rated engines to choose from in 1972. That list included the standard ZQ-3 350, the LT-1 and the LS-5 454. Advertised output for the latter was now down to 270 horsepower, although you would have never known it by looking beneath the hood. For the first time a Corvette big-block carried no horsepower label on its air cleaner lid. Customers in California in 1972 were none the wiser since they didn't even get a look at that lid. Chevrolet officials that year didn't feel it necessary to take the time to put the LS-5 through that state's stringent emissions testing, meaning it failed to meet certification for sale there in 1972. It wouldn't be the first time that a Corvette engine would be "banned" on the West Coast.

Corvettes built from 1970 to 1973 featured rectangular exhaust outlets, as opposed to the rounded units used in 1968–69. This 1972 coupe represents the last of the breed with chrome front bumpers. The luggage rack was a popular dealer-installed option. Standard power comes from the 200-horsepower 350 small-block.

As for the rest of the 1968–72 drivetrain, the plot wasn't nearly as thick. Optional transmissions for 1968 rolled over from 1967 with one exception. The obsolete two-speed Power-glide automatic, RPO M35, was finally super-seded by Chevrolet's excellent three-speed Turbo Hydra-Matic, which had first appeared in 1965. The M40 Turbo Hydra-Matic was made available behind the 1968 Corvette's base 327 as well as the two hydraulic-lifter 427s, the L-36 and L-68. The M35 option in 1967 was priced at $194.35. The M40 in 1968 cost $226.45.

As in 1967, the L-79 small-block was only offered with a four-speed stick, as were the me-chanically cammed L-71 and L-88 brutes. Three Muncie four-speeds were again listed: along with the M21 close-ratio (with its 2.20:1 low gear), there was the M20 wide-ratio (2.52:1 low) box and the bullet-proof M22 "Rock Crusher." Both the M20 and M21 were priced at $184.35 in 1968, and either could've been bolted up to the L-79 327, L-36 427, or L-68 427. As mentioned, L-71 installations were lim-ited to the M21, while the M22 was mated only to the L-88, and vice-versa.

Those last two arrangements changed in 1969 when Chevrolet made the tough Turbo Hydra-Matic available behind the two solid-lifter 427s, and not a moment too soon in some minds. "The Turbo Hydro is the best thing that's happened to big-engined Corvettes since high-octane gas," wrote *Hot Rod*'s Steve Kelly. "Those who can overcome the four-speed mystique are in for a surprise" claimed *Car Life*'s Corvette fans. "The Turbo Hydra-Matic fitted to the high-performance 427s is magnificent. It slips from gear to gear in traffic without so much as a nudge. Power tight-ens the shifts into a series of iron hands, strong enough to light the tires at every change."

When ordered with the base 350 that year, the M40 option was priced at $221.80. It cost $290.40 when mated to the L-71 or L-88. "In the mild engine, the M40 was set to shift up quickly," continued *Car Life*'s July 1969 L-88/automatic review. "In the wild engines, the transmission stays in the lower gear until the driver lifts his foot, right up to redline." Availability of the T.H. automatic continued for the 454 big-blocks, both the LS-5 and LS-6. But it never made it into the LT-1 small-block's realm.

Bringing up the rear in 1968 was the G81 Positraction differential in most cases. Priced at $46.35, the G81 axle was a mandatory extra-cost choice behind all engine/trans combos save for the manual-shifted 327s. Positraction truly was optional for those latter combinations, which came standard with an open differential. The same situation carried over into 1969 before the obvious conclusion was finally reached: Positraction represented the only way to take off. Mandated or not, RPO G81 installations had been on the rise throughout the 1960s. In 1963 the Positraction percentage was 81.6. It was 88.5 in 1967, 94.5 in 1968, and 95.4 in 1969. That figure became 100 percent in 1970 when "posi" gears were made standard equipment on all Corvettes regardless of engine or trannie.

A similar situation occurred involving the third-generation Corvette's standard transmission. Three-speed sticks were for wimps. Real men (or women) demanded four on the floor, and had done so in ever-increasing numbers every year since Chevrolet first offered an optional four-speed to Corvette buyers in 1957. Three-speed Corvettes that year made up 67.5 percent of the mix, automatics 22, four-gears only 10.5. In 1958 the breakdown was 43.1 percent three-speeds, 34.5 fours. Four-speeds then gained the majority the following year, 43.2 percent to 37.4. By 1961, three-speeds were making up only 22.6 percent of the production run. That figure fell to 4.3 in 1963. A mere 1.9 percent of the market stuck with the standard gearbox in 1967, followed by 1.1 percent in 1968.

By this point many Chevrolet dealers were shying away from the rarely made requests for a base three-speed model in fear of being stuck themselves should the buyer back out of the deal. Such requests were answered only 0.6 percent of the time in 1969. Of the record 38,762 Corvettes built that year, a mere 252 hit the streets with three-speeds. Not enough was enough.

In 1970 the M20 wide-ratio four-speed transmission joined the Positraction rear axle on the Corvette's standard equipment list as the three-speed was finally shelved next to the old Powerglide automatic. Both the close-ratio M21 manual box and the Turbo Hydra-Matic automatic could've been ordered in place of the M20 at no extra cost. Yet another former option, tinted glass all around, also was tossed in as part of the standard deal in 1970.

Of course anyone who thought this new deal was a deal had another thing coming. Before 1970, Corvette buyers got what they paid for. After 1970, they paid for what they got. Adding equipment that previously cost extra into the standard package meant simply that Chevrolet had to ask more for that package. After increasing only 2.5 percent from 1968 to 1969, the Corvette coupe's base price jumped 8.6 percent in 1970. And with that jump, the 1970 coupe became the first Corvette to wear a $5,000 standard sticker. The actual figure was $5,192. After coming in at $4,849 in 1970, the Corvette convertible too reached the five-grand plateau in 1971. Its base price that year was $5,259.

John DeLorean and crew at Chevrolet couldn't be blamed for these price hikes. There was nothing personal involved, it was simply good business. Corvette demand was as high as ever as the 1970s dawned. Why not keep charging customers more and more until someone said stop? Buyers proved each year that they wanted more out of their Corvette and they were willing to pay whatever "more" cost. Thus the reasoning behind the addition of more and more standard features. Although many among the sport-conscious press cringed at the direction the third-generation Corvette was taking, it was clear to Chevy execs that adding toys was the best way to go. And who cared if those toys raised the bottom line by leaps and bounds?

Demand for comfort and convenience items like air conditioning, power brakes and steering, and automatic transmission skyrocketed in the early 1970s. This in turn meant that fewer and fewer Corvettes sold were going for anywhere close to those five-grand base stickers. The 454 coupe *Road & Track* tested in 1970 carried a $6,773 price tag. And with a full load of extras, it also carried 3,740 pounds, 47 percent of which rested lightly on the rear wheels. Little wonder that this 390-horsepower Turbo Hydra-Matic Corvette needed 15 seconds to reach the far end of the quarter-mile. And its nose-heavy, luxury-liner nature left few doubts as to what conclusions *R&T*'s critics would make. "The 7.4-liter automatic Corvette was one of the better Corvettes we've driven lately," they began, "but its great weight and incompetence on any but the smoothest roads keep it from being an outstanding GT or sports car."

Maybe so. But by then America's only sports car was well on its way to becoming every bit as much a luxury GT as it was a performance machine. And as horsepower waned further after 1972, the Corvette's softer side grew even more apparent.

PUTTING THE *BIG* IN BIG-BLOCK
Legends Labeled L-88, ZL-1 and LS-6

Not until the arrival of the technologically advanced ZR-1 in 1990 would Corvette drivers find themselves flexing their muscles as strongly as they did during the Shark years. Yet even with dual overhead cams, four valves per cylinder and microprocessor-controlled fuel injection, the 375-horsepower LT5 V-8 could still "only" motivate the first ZR-1s through the quarter-mile in 13 seconds plus a few tenths. Mind you, that much awesome speed was certainly nothing to sneeze at. Nor were the 405 horses unleashed by some extra headwork performed on the high-tech LT5 in 1993. Nonetheless, neither the 375- nor 405-horsepower ZR-1 could claim the crown of the quickest Vette yet.

That honor still belongs to the big-block Corvettes of yore, those fire-breathing, gas-gulping, tire-torturing monster rats that only could have roamed the earth in the days before catalytic converters, 5-mile-per-hour bumpers, and corporate-average-fuel-economy ratings. These beastly rodents only survived for 10 years, which is actually stretching it when you consider that the "smog motor" examples in 1972, 1973, and 1974 were mere shadows of their former selves. The pre-1972 persona was another story entirely. In those days, rat-motored Corvettes ran at the head of the pack with Detroit's most powerful performance machines. This was a direct result of Zora Duntov's willingness to push the outside of Chevrolet's existing performance envelope as far as it would go, even if that meant leading the Corvette away from the world-class sports car ideal he reportedly preferred.

"It is known that Duntov is a great exponent of small-displacement, high-revving engines, and it would seem logical that he would be pushing for the manufacture of smaller, lighter Corvettes powered by the zappy, exciting, 302 ci Z/28 engine," explained a 1969 *Car and Driver* report. "But here Duntov faces a difficult personal choice. Because he rightfully believes that his Corvette should represent the pinnacle of Chevrolet engineering, he cannot bring himself to accept producing his car with anything less than the biggest, most powerful engine in the Chevrolet lineup. He feels, with some justification, that it would be absurd to market a 305- or 350-ci Corvette as the top performance car in the division when a customer could buy a Chevelle or Chevy II with a much larger and more powerful engine. Therefore he consents to his once-nimble machine being made bulkier and bulkier by the year."

Compared to the compact, lightweight, all-aluminum LT5, the bulky, cranky, iron-block Mk IV V-8s of the 1960s and 1970s were decidedly low-tech, what with their all-or-nothing carburetors and those conventional pushrods typically operating 16 valves. But relatively speaking, all things are not always equal. Sure, you can call the Mk IV a yeoman powerplant from today's perspective. However, we hope you did so with a smile, mister, 30 years ago if you were driving a big-block musclecar from Ford or Chrysler. Be it 426 Hemi or Boss 429, you still would've been left behind wearing a sheepish grin if you dared take on the hottest of the Mk IV Corvettes.

Zora Duntov rolled out the first race-ready L-88 Corvette in 1967. This L-88, one of 20 built that year, is possibly the first of that run. Notice the unique "L-88" decal on the scoop—no other L-88 was known to have special exterior identification. Racing exhausts are also included here.

Special identification is also found beneath the hood of this particular 1967 L-88 Corvette. Notice the road draft tube (black fitting exiting valve cover just behind "L/88" decal)—smog controls didn't "come into vogue" nationally until 1968. L-88s built for 1967 were totally devoid of emissions hardware.

In 1966 a *Car and Driver* road test posted an incredible 12.8-second E.T. for the first 427 Vette. Any faster than that in a street car and you would be . . . well, you probably would be fibbing because street cars simply do not run that fast. Not with full exhausts, standard tires, and 3,500 pounds of body, engine, frame, heater, radio, and so on.

The key term here is *street car*. When Zora was stretching the envelope 30 years ago he had no qualms about putting what were basically racing machines on the street. "Basically" racing machines? No ifs, ands, or buts about it, the legendary L-88 and ZL-1 Corvettes were never intended to simply relocate drivers or passengers from point A to B. Don't let those compliant air pumps used in 1968 and 1969 fool you. The aluminum-head L-88 427 and its all-aluminum ZL-1 brother were built only to run fast. Fast at the track.

That's undoubtedly where all of the first L-88s built in 1967 ended up. Nowhere were these cars promoted to the general public for general use. Nor were they legal for such use due to the fact that they were totally devoid of even the simplest of emission-control devices. And considering that only 20 were sold, it's a fair bet that they were claimed by "insiders" who were well aware of the L-88's intentions, as

well as Duntov's. He was counting on the L-88s to promote the Corvette image in sanctioned competition, and he wanted serious racers—customers able to make the right modifications needed to maximize this exotic big-block's full potential—to be the ones doing the taking.

Efforts to guarantee the latter included downplaying the L-88's image, both on paper and in actual physical presence. Outwardly, the first L-88 Corvette looked like any other big-block Sting Ray built in 1967. Save for the distinctive hood (that no one could miss) added the following year, much the same could be said for the 1968 and 1969 L-88s. No specific exterior identification was ever added, this of course to help keep Duntov's not-so-little secret a secret.

"One of the factory's ways to discourage casual buying of L-88s is not to supply a little badge on the fender for the unfortunate many to see and envy," explained *Car Life*'s snitches later in 1969. "The L-88 is the only performance car on the American market we can think of without one."

Another factory ploy involved advertised output. According to Chevrolet paperwork, the L-88 produced 430 horsepower at 5,200 rpm. This claim wasn't necessarily a lie, it just didn't tell the whole story. L-88 427s were delivered from the factory with standard Mk IV exhaust manifolds dumping into a standard dual exhaust system. Duntov and crew knew full well that the first thing a racer would do was deep-six the whole works in favor of wide-open headers. Most in the know agreed that this typical modification alone instantly freed up at least 100 horses. As Chevrolet engineer Fred Frincke later told it, early dyno tests of an L-88 fitted with free-breathing tube headers in place of those stock cast-iron manifolds resulted in a much more realistic figure, as much as 550 horsepower.

Clearly Chevy's promotional pencil-pushers could've never advertised that many horses and not drawn the ire of watchdogs both inside and out of GM. Look what happened when Chevrolet tried to print 450-horsepower decals for the L-72 427 in 1966. That number was erased and 425 was written in before the L-72 was released, apparently because that original label would have offended sensibilities. Or safety crusaders.

Nor did Duntov want such big, bold numbers attracting the attention of Walter Mitty types, they with too many dollars and too few brains. The hope was that Walter and friends would overlook the L-88—it with its "mere" 430 horses—and go for the L-71 with its lineup-leading 435-horsepower decal.

So what was the truth? Chevrolet continued publishing that 430-horsepower figure in 1968 and 1969 even after various upgrades were made. Along with beefier connecting rods, changes in 1968 included a new standard cam (various other over-the-counter bumpsticks were listed in 1968 and 1969) and the midyear addition of Chevy's famed open-chamber heads. Revised cam specs were 347 degrees duration on the intake side, 364 on the exhaust, with 136 degrees of overlap. Lift was 0.5586-inch intake, 0.580 exhaust. L-88 torque output in 1968 was listed as 485 ft-lb at 4,000 rpm. In 1969 it was 450 ft-lb at 4,400 rpm.

Twenty-three years later, *Corvette Fever* published dynamometer test results for a correctly restored/rebuilt L-88. At 4,400 rpm, it was churning out 502 ft-lb of torque. Maximum torque was actually 513 ft-lb at 4,200 turns. As for horsepower, at 5,200 revs the score actually read 489. But that wasn't all. What Chevrolet's little white lies also failed to mention was that 5,200 wasn't the power peak. According to *Corvette Fever*'s 1992 test,

the L-88's true maximum output of 514 horses arrived at 6,200 revolutions.

Even a blind man could see that these numbers ran well beyond the realm of anything considered a "street car." Yet that still didn't stop some armchair racers dead set on taking an L-88 to the streets. Sales of Chevrolet's wildest Corvette jumped considerably once word got out. Production of L-88s—both coupes and convertibles—reached 80 in 1968. Another 116 arrived in 1969, including 17 equipped with Turbo Hydra-Matic automatics instead of four-speeds.

How many of these actually went from the delivery truck directly to the track? Certainly not all. Unlike the emissions-illegal 1967 L-88, the 1968 and 1969 renditions were fitted with full smog controls, including a PCV valve and Chevrolet's Air Injection Reaction system. Adding the AIR air pump simply made it too easy for Mr. Mitty to try street racing an L-88. Some undoubtedly even tried driving one down to the store. How many of these actually made it to point B? Certainly not all.

Car Life explained the situation in 1969. "Duntov asked that somebody try to get his message across: The L-88 is being bought by

Zora Duntov and Denny Davis keep a watchful eye on an early L-88 427 during dyno testing in May 1966. *Chevrolet Motor Division*

While there was no special exterior badging, L-88 Corvettes built in 1968 and 1969 couldn't be missed with their functional air-induction hoods. Only 80 L-88s were built in 1968, including this coupe. Another 116 followed in 1969. *Tom Glatch*

people who don't know what it is and don't know or care to use it properly. They hear it's the hot thing to have, and that the factory doesn't put L-88 on the order blank, so they order one." They also ordered more than their fair share of headaches. An L-88 Corvette truly was "the hot thing to have," in more ways than one.

If a speed freak wanted to drive one of these unforgiving big-blocks in everyday traffic, it was his prerogative. After all, it was once a free country, right? Free, too, for the foolish. "The L-88, even in showroom form, is closer to being a racer than a cruiser," wrote *Hot Rod*'s Steve Kelly, "and it would seem almost sacrilegious to see an L-88 'Vette serving duty as a transportation machine only." It also would seem almost stupid considering that, as Chevrolet paperwork officially explained, the L-88 was clearly "not intended for street use." As if Chevy had to tell us.

From top to bottom, this purpose-built, off-road powerplant was good to go, and go like no Corvette V-8 ever had before. L-88 roots traced back to 1965 when engineers Frincke, Cal Wade, and Denny Davis began putting together a collection of race-ready big-block parts. These parts then went together to form the foundation for a competition-legal production Corvette that Duntov hoped would pick up

where his ill-fated Grand Sports left off. Although Chevrolet wasn't supposed to be in racing—the GM upper office edict that had squelched the Grand Sport project early in 1963 had reportedly decided all that—Zora wasn't about to give up without a fight. He had an L-88 427 running on a dyno as early as October 1965, and he hoped to release it as a Corvette option in 1966.

By then rumors among the press were already doing their own running, rampant-style. *Sports Car Graphic*'s Jerry Titus—one of Duntov's favorite journalists—was among the first to report news of the L-88's impending arrival in *SCG*'s March 1965 issue. "Among the options that will make the [Corvette] competitive is a new four-speed gearbox designed to handle a 'prodified' [read: homologated] version of the [Mk IV] engine," wrote Titus. "An estimated 470 horsepower is expected [for this engine] with application of allowable SCCA modifications." The transmission Titus referred to was the M22 Rock Crusher, which got its nickname from the noises emitted by its big, burly, nearly straight-cut gears. This bulletproof box made it into production as an extra-heavy-duty option in 1966, and would remain the only real racer's choice behind the Corvette's most brutal V-8s up through 1972.

Duntov did file L-88 homologation papers with the Sports Car Club of America and the Federation International de L'Automobile (FIA, the governing body of international racing) in late 1965. And various L-88 components did make it into Roger Penske's hands in 1966. However, RPO L-88 wasn't officially released until early 1967. Originally priced at $947.90, the L-88 427 was complemented by an impressive array of mandatory "options" that ran the bill up even higher. Along with the M22 four-speed, L-88 accompaniment included the K66 transistorized ignition, J56 power-assisted metallic brakes, F41 heavy-duty suspension, and G81 Positraction axle.

Most impressive, though, was the L-88 itself. Beginning with the already stout Mk IV cylinder block with its four-bolt main bearing caps, this competition-bred 427 was fitted with a special crankshaft forged out of 5140 alloy steel, cross-drilled for ample lubrication and tuftrided for hardness. Shot-peened, magnafluxed connecting rods were attached to that crank. At the business ends of those rods were

eight forged-aluminum pop-up pistons that could almost split atoms at the resulting 12.5:1 compression ratio. Topping off the L-88's iron block was a pair of weight-saving aluminum heads fitted with large valves: 2.19-inches on the intake side, 1.84 on the exhaust.

Supplying fuel/air to this righteous rat was a huge 850-cubic-feet-per-minute Holley four-barrel. The special high-rise aluminum intake below that carb had its internal partition machined down to create an open plenum for maximum high-rpm performance. Initial specs for Denny Davis' radical solid-lifter cam listed lift at 0.5365 inch for the intake valve, 0.5560 for the exhaust. Duration was 337 degrees intake, 340 exhaust. Thickened 7/16-inch pushrods with hardened ends delivered that lift to those big valves through "long-slot" stamped steel rocker arms rocking on heat-treated, hardened ball-studs. Heavy-duty valve springs were held in place by reinforced retainers and locks.

On the L-88's breathing end, a unique "air cleaner" (using the term very loosely) fit into ductwork in the hood's underside. That duct ran back to the hood's trailing edge where it drew in cooler, denser air from the high-pressure area at the base of the windshield. The L-88s of 1967–69 (along with the 1969 ZL-1) were the only Corvettes fitted with a functional air-induction

hood prior to the 1973 introduction of a similar standard-equipment design. And thanks to the extra clearance supplied by that big, bulging rear-facing hood scoop, the L-88 and ZL-1 were the only big-block Corvettes built after 1967 that weren't required to switch over to the low-rise intake manifold necessitated by the Shark body's low hoodline.

Between the L-88 and M22 was an appropriate heavy-duty clutch mated to a small 12.75-inch-diameter flywheel, the latter added in the best interests of increasing rpm potential by reducing reciprocating mass. Cooling came by way of a Harrison heavy-duty cross-flow radiator. Cooling actually came barely by way of this aluminum radiator due to the fact that it wasn't fitted with a fan shroud to help maximize efficiency whenever the tach needle was low to the left. On its own, that missing shroud represented warning enough from the factory against putting the L-88 to use on the street.

At a glance, the aluminum-head 427's off-road status was especially evident during its first year in production. Even if you weren't aware of the L-88's sky-high compression or didn't understand that a big-block Corvette really, really needed that shroud to keep things cool at low rpm, you couldn't miss the "chicken-wire" screen atop the carburetor or that road-draft

The most exotic Corvette ever unleashed "on the street" was the 1969 ZL-1. The all-aluminum 427 V-8 lurking beneath that big ZL-2 hood was also jokingly rated at 430 horsepower.

Duntov brought a collection of wild Corvettes to 1969 press leads, including this white ZL-1 convertible. Fitted with fender flares and extra-wide wheels, this road rocket gave *Motor Trend*'s Eric Dalhquist (driving here) the ride of his life. Quarter-mile times were about 11-seconds flat. *Used with permission of EMAP/Petersen Publishing,* Motor Trend *magazine*

tube exiting the driver-side valve cover in place of the environmentally correct positive crankcase ventilation system. As you might guess, most race cars avoid inhibiting airflow into the engine with a conventional filter. And they don't need a fan, let alone a shroud, since they rarely get stuck in traffic. Nor are they required to meet federally mandated emissions standards, thus the explanation for the 1967 L-88's inconsiderate venting of crankcase vapors directly into the atmosphere via that draft tube.

Also inconsiderate was the 1967 L-88's interior accommodations. RPO C48, the heater-defroster delete credit offered to Sting Ray buyers from 1963 to 1967, was included as part of the original L-88 deal. Radios were unavailable as well. Same for all other extra-cost creature comforts. The only addition made inside was a label stuck onto the console. It read, "Warning: vehicle must operate on a fuel having a minimum of 103 research octane and 95 motor octane or engine damage may result." "Under no circumstances should regular gasoline be used," reiterated an L-88's delivery paperwork.

Fouling the air, battling that inherent hot temper, paying extra for jet fuel, and cruising without tunes weren't the only hurdles put before those brave souls who dared try to domesticate the wild and wooly L-88. Their task proved daunting enough immediately after turning the key. A lot of fancy footwork followed during cold starts due to the absence of a choke. And even when Chevrolet's retrofit choke kit was added to that enormous four-barrel, the L-88 427 still didn't like to cooperate as its cavernous intake and lumpy, loping cam totally sacrificed low-rpm operation for all-out high-rev usage. Idle speed was a teeth-chattering 1,000 rpm. Automatic L-88s in 1969 were commonly set to idle at two-grand, making shifts out of park a surprising experience unless both feet weren't firmly squashing the brake pedal.

The sum of these parts added up to the wildest V-8 ever put on the street—the ZL-1 427. Notice the big Holley double-pumper, the open-plenum intake, and those open-chamber heads with their huge, round exhaust ports. *Chevrolet Motor Division*

All this and some jet-setters still didn't get the picture.

"The L-88 is supposed to be a competition car," explained *Car Life*'s 1969 review of five of the six (the L-89/L-71 was tested, the ZL-1 wasn't) 427 Corvettes offered that year. "Racers remove everything they don't need. Duntov saves them as much trouble as he can by not putting on anything that competition or the government don't require. There's no radiator shroud, because it isn't needed at high speed."

Of course Duntov's engineers easily could have bolted up a typical shroud to the L-88's Harrison radiator—if, that is, they gave a spit about enhancing low-speed operation. As you already know, they didn't. And even when street-wise owners turned the wrench themselves, the L-88's high-compression furnaces still kept things too hot to handle. "The owner of a rental fleet in St. Louis has a shop full of L-88s, which overheat constantly in traffic," continued *Car Life*. "He wishes Duntov would do something. Duntov wishes people wouldn't buy racing cars for use in cities."

The ZL-1's aluminum block was cast with extra material on the bottom end to help hold up like its cast-iron brethren. Those are iron liners in the cylinder bores. Notice the extra "ears" atop each cylinder bank deck. They were added specially to the aluminum casting and drilled for an extra pair of cylinder head bolts to tighten the grip between block and head. *Chevrolet Motor Division*

Although many similarities did exist, simply calling the ZL-1 427 an L-88 with a block made of aluminum instead of iron is not correct. The block itself was an entirely different animal as it had to be specially beefed-up to make up for its less-durable aluminum construction. Behind the 1969 ZL-1 here is a 1967 L-88.

Zora himself was the first to admit that street performance was by no means the L-88 Corvette's forte, especially so in pure-stock form with those spoil-sport cast-iron exhausts. "The horsepower ratings tell the story," added *Car Life*. "Camshafts in the higher rated L-71 and L-89 are designed to give maximum power through the stock exhaust manifolds and mufflers. The L-88 cam is designed to give maximum power, period. It won't give all it has got unless, and until, it has tuned exhaust headers blasting unmuffled into the air."

With socially acceptable mufflers and its optional removable top in place, the auto-trans L-88 convertible *Car Life* tested in 1969 tripped the lights in 14.10 seconds at 106.9 miles per hour, this with a less-than-desirable 3.36:1 rear axle. But while those economy-minded gears sacrificed the car's off-the-line abilities, they naturally assisted things on the top end. At a rod-knocking 6,800 rpm, the L-88's maximum velocity registered at 151 miles per hour.

Hot Rod's Steve Kelly reported better dragstrip results with the same L-88 convertible. He also noted even more potential. "The tall gear in back made 13.56 seconds at 111 miles per

hour seem respectable," wrote Kelly in *HRM*'s April 1969 issue. "But we know it's two seconds from where it should be."

The 1969 L-88 was right at the top in another performance category. The weight reduction up front—created by adding those aluminum heads—working in concert with the mandatory heavy-duty F41 suspension, made the L-88 Corvette, in Kelly's words, "the best-handling car built in this country." This was "one U.S. car that'll compete with any $10,000 European, and do it with less money involved," he concluded.

Of course what he failed to mention was that much the same could be said about the L-89 Corvette, as it also featured lightweight aluminum heads and the heavyweight F41 underpinnings. And at $832.15, the L-89 option meant even less money was involved. The tag for RPO L-88 in 1969 was $1,032.15. Furthermore, the 435-horse L-89 Corvette was a street car, it could make it down to the store. And back. In fast enough fashion to suit any card-carrying Walter Mitty club member to a T. The choice was yours. The "L-88 had more potential, but the buyer must extract it for himself," began *Car Life*'s conclusion. "The L-89 was designed to be the hottest Corvette in street trim."

There are those words again. In *street trim* the hottest Corvette of all time was the aforementioned 12.8-second L-72 427 of 1966. The hottest third-generation Corvette? The bodacious tri-carb L-71 and its low-weight, high-priced L-89 derivative of 1968 and 1969 commonly won magazine road test derbies with elapsed times running well into the 13-second range. Yikes.

Take away that "street" qualification and the numbers became even more scary. The L-88, of course, would have beaten everything in sight had Chevrolet public relations people been more willing to show it off. Not only did they not make a test vehicle available to the press until 1969, they also went out of their way to limit results—remember the automatic trans and 3.36:1 gears? Even with its restrictive exhausts, a four-speed L-88 (Turbo Hydra-Matic cars were limited to 2.73:1, 3.08:1, or 3.36:1 differentials only) undoubtedly would have eclipsed the 1966 L-72's record with only a switch to the 4.11:1 optional axle. The stump-pulling 4.56:1 cogs would have salted away the deal without question.

WARNING: VEHICLE MUST OPERATE ON A FUEL HAVING OF MINIMUM RESEARCH 103 AND MOTOR OCTANE OR 95 OCTANE ENGINE MAY DAMAGE RESULT

A driver was given fair warning if he dared take a ZL-1 to the streets in 1969. Even if you missed the small console tag, you couldn't help but read the red letters, upside-down or otherwise.

And to think the L-88 still didn't represent the tip of the thermometer in 1969. The hottest Corvette that year—the hottest Corvette to ever make an RPO list, period—was the incredible ZL-1. Why stop there? Never before or since has an American automaker dared deliver so much raw power to the people. Yes, John Q. Public could have walked into his neighborhood Chevy dealership in 1969 and rolled out in a street-legal, emissions-controlled 427 Corvette able to break not simply into the 13-second bracket. Nor the 12. Breaking the sound barrier was more like it.

In July 1968, Zora Duntov and his merry band of speed merchants showed up at the 1969 new model press introduction with two sinister-looking Corvettes; both wearing the familiar ZL-2 air-induction hood already made famous by the L-88. Journalists on hand even figured they were looking at "just" another aluminum-head 427 beneath those bulging hoods because, unlike "regular-production" all-aluminum ZL-1 big-blocks, these test mule engines featured painted cylinder blocks. "All those guys at the 1969 Chevy preview thought it was an L-88," explained a December 1968 *Hot Rod* introduction of Chevrolet's "Better Mousetrap." "Forgot your pocket magnets, right guys?"

What they didn't forget was a big right foot.

Neither one of these mules could've been mistaken for street cars. One was a white convertible with huge, wide-open sidepipes below each door and imposing fender flares at all four corners housing super-fat Firestone treads. Set up by Zora himself, this car was equipped for road-racing duty. Behind its aluminum big-block was a Rock Crusher four-speed that delivered torque to relatively tall 3.70:1 gears out back. Even with those "road gears," this ZL-1 mule was rarin' to run from rest to however fast you wanted to go in a major hurry.

"The ZL-1 doesn't just accelerate, because the word 'accelerate' is inadequate for this car," wrote *Motor Trend*'s Eric Dahlquist after a ride in that great, white whale of a Corvette. "It tears its way through the air and across the black pavement like all the modern big-inch racing machines you have ever seen, the engine climbing the rev band in that leaping gait as the tires hunt for traction, find it, lose it again for a millisecond, then find it until they are locked in."

Once locked in, those racing Firestones propelled Duntov's white ZL-1 through the quarter in 12.1 seconds at 116 miles per hour. Dahlquist also mentioned roaring from 30 miles per hour to 145 (at 6,500 rpm) in what he estimated to be about 1,700 feet. "If the car had a higher gear, one of the engineers casually mentions, it

Tom Langdon and Gib Hufstader built this orange 1969 coupe to especially impress journalists at the 1969 new car introductions. It returned in slightly different form in 1970. The first year, it showcased a ZL-1 V-8. In 1970, it was powered by the LT-2, the 454-ci all-aluminum derivative of the ZL-1. With wide-open headers, slicks, and a high-stall Turbo Hydra-Matic, the car could bolt through the quarter-mile in nearly 10.5 seconds. *Gib Hufstader*

will bust 195, possibly 200," he added. A lower gear (higher numerically) would have easily translated into 11 seconds in the quarter mile. If not less.

Journalists themselves were invited to take the other mule's reins—and hang on for dear life. Created by developmental engineers Gib Hufstader and Tom Langdon, this flaming orange (contemporary magazine reports called it red) coupe was an entirely different animal. "Tom built the engine, I built the car," remembered Hufstader in 1999. "He got about 710 horsepower out of it. I took out all the steel body reinforcement and made the bumper out of fiberglass and chrome plated it, anything to help get the weight down."

Hufstader and Langdon's lightweight ZL-1 coupe featured headers, sidepipes, a special beefed-up, high-stall Turbo Hydra-Matic automatic,

4.88:1 dragstrip gears, and 9-inch racing slicks. Once in the hands of the press, the car's auto-box allowed even the meekest, mild-mannered member of the fourth estate to run faster than a speeding bullet without even breaking a sweat. Or at least it felt that way.

"Twenty or 30 people were given the chance to drive this really high-performance car," said Hufstader. "They all had a great time." "It was a terrific machine," added Proving Grounds public relations man Bob Clift. "We all enjoyed driving it. That was back in the good ol' days. Zora used to keep us all excited back then."

Anyone strapped into that orange Corvette on that summer day in July 1968 came away from the experience ecstatic. Running 11-flat through the quarter-mile at about 127 miles per hour was as easy as stomping the go-pedal and

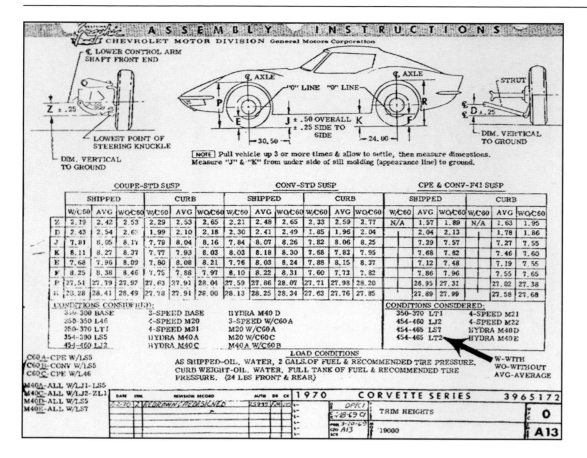

This page from the 1970 Corvette assembly manual lists the LT-2, LS-7, and LJ-2 454s. The LT-2 was supposed to follow in the ZL-1's tracks, the LS-7 in the L-88's. The LJ-2 was intended to replace the triple-carb 427. An LJ-1 is also listed. Could this have been the 3x2 L-68's second coming? Or did the LJ-2 plan include aluminum heads, meaning it was meant to replace the L-89/L-71? If so, then the LJ-1 may have been the iron-head tri-carb 454 version of the L-71 427.

pointing the high-rising hood in the right direction. Even quicker runs were posted by applying a little street-racer know-how. "We were revving it up to 6,000 [rpm] then dumping it into gear," recalled Clift with a chuckle. "It took off like a striped-ass ape." The best time slip of the day read 10.89 seconds at 130 miles per hour. But all that excitement almost ended up in a downer.

"They got the car back to the shop after [press day] and found many stress cracks where the flywheel attached to the crank," added Clift. "It probably would've come apart after a few more runs. As it was, we did 20 or 30 passes like that, banging the shifts into drive. If it had blown up, that wouldn't have been so great for a press introduction."

Though they nearly tortured it to death, that ZL-1 coupe showed most of those journalists the hottest time they'd ever had behind the wheel of an American automobile. Ten-eighty-nine wasn't just fast, it was ridiculous. Ridiculously easy. "The fact that almost anybody who knows how to drive could jump in and duplicate this run after run may be the most shattering as-

pect of all," concluded a *Motor Trend* report entitled "The 10-second Trip."

Altered by hallucinogens or not, why anyone in his right mind would want to tear across the pavement that quickly also begged the question of what type of maniac in 1969 would fall in line to buy a ZL-1 Corvette? "First, he will have a lot of money," answered Duntov 30 years ago. A potential customer would've probably needed to have a spare Cadillac lying around because, like its L-88 cousin, the ZL-1 was best (make that only) suited for off-road use. Beyond that, RPO ZL-1 alone cost $4,718.35. For another 70 bucks or so, John Q. could have ordered a standard 300-horsepower 350 small-block that year—and it would have arrived on Mr. Public's doorstep wrapped in a 1969 Corvette coupe. A ballpark bottom-line for the complete ZL-1 Corvette package neared $10,000.

While nine- or ten-grand is still not exactly chump-change today, it was some seriously mean green in 1969, especially for a car as narrow-focused as the ZL-1. Was it worth it? Eric Dahlquist thought so. Calling the car "the first

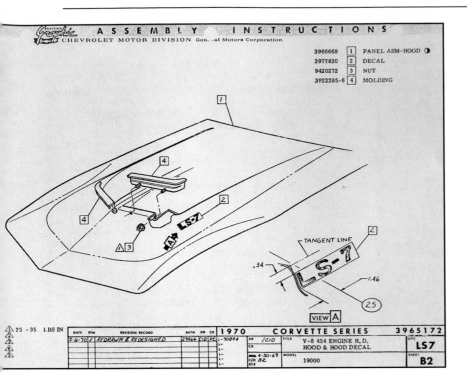

ASSEMBLY INSTRUCTIONS
CHEVROLET MOTOR DIVISION Gen..al Motors Corporation

3966669	1	PANEL ASM-HOOD
3977830	2	DECAL
9420272	3	NUT
3922285-6	4	MOLDING

TANGENT LINE

.34

LS-7

1.46

25

VIEW A

25 - 35 LBS IN

DATE	SYM	REVISION RECORD	AUTH DR OR CK	1970		CORVETTE SERIES		3965172
5-6-70	1	REDRAWN & REDESIGNED	29464 CID HC	L-70844	DR /CID	TITLE V-8 454 ENGINE H.D. HOOD & HOOD DECAL	UPC	LS7
					CX			
				APPD 4-30-69			SHEET	
				CJO B2	MODEL			B2
				ECR	19000			

An assembly manual page was devoted to the LS-7 hood's special identification. While small-block fans were treated to a decal denoting the LT-1's presence, no production Corvette big-block (save for perhaps the 1967 L-88 shown on these pages) was ever labeled with anything other than a displacement badge.

American Ferrari," he explained that "you must pay a price for the ZL-1 excellence and it is quite high. [But] considering that an L-88 Corvette goes for $6,000, a $9,000 ZL-1 tab is a reasonable figure. You're going to sell every [ZL-1] you make anyway and your nearest competition is twice as much so why not show the gang in Modena they're not alone anymore?"

In Dahlquist's learned opinion, Duntov indeed had finally done it; he had fathered a world-class Corvette capable of running with Europe's finest sports cars. "They said Detroit could never build anything like a Ferrari because some product planning committee or cost accounting group would pinpoint the economic folly of such low-volume madness, compromise it and send it on to the world just another gimmicked-up cop out," he wrote in *Motor Trend*'s May 1969 issue. "But Duntov, the man, is Man in his old, pure, adventuresome, non-vinyl person, and that's why he was able to create an American Ferrari that is not even partially contemporary Woolworth."

Eric Dahlquist knew American performance cars, and he was convinced that the ZL-1 Corvette represented the ultimate rendition of such. Not only could it run away from anything on wheels (and perhaps a few things with wings), it could do so in the curves as well as down the straightaway. "It is the best handling

Corvette ever built," he concluded—which in turn meant it was the best handling American car ever built. "With a 43/57 front to rear weight distribution, the 2,808-pound car is almost neutral with just a shade of understeer that you can overpower at will with the throttle."

Lowered weight, both in total and up front, was, of course, the key to the ZL-1's incredibly well-balanced performance. This was indeed a Corvette that offered the best of both worlds—big-block brute force and small-block nimbleness. In fact, the big, brawny ZL-1 even did its 350-powered brethren one better. Weight-saving aluminum heads on the L-88 and L-89 427s helped those two big-blocks carry only about 60 pounds more than a typical 350 small-block. With an aluminum cylinder block to go with those feather-light heads, the ZL-1 V-8 amazingly tipped the scales at roughly 25 pounds less than a 350.

Duntov may have been, in *Car and Driver*'s words, "a great exponent of small-displacement, high-revving engines." But he also loved his horsepower. "Zora was always anxious for more of everything," explained Gib Hufstader when asked how the ZL-1 fit in with Duntov's ideal for the supreme American sports car. "But the real sin was that people never did buy them." Clearly Dahlquist's justifications couldn't sway wealthy jet-setters who apparently felt the $9,000 ZL-1 tab was an unreasonable figure. "It was a different economy back then," added Hufstader. "People weren't throwing money at cars like they do today. No one wanted to spend that much for just an engine."

Almost no one. Reportedly RPO ZL-1 was checked off twice in 1969.

Explaining how other ZL-1 Corvettes have been spotted over the years is easy enough. Legend has it that as many as 5 test mules or executive toys were built. Some claims say 10 to 12. It then follows that 1 or more of these may have survived, with or without their original engines—probably the latter. And being race-ready powerplants, both the L-88 and ZL-1 427s were also offered individually "in a crate" to racers, professionally or otherwise. It logically follows further that the possibility existed for any number of these crate-motor ZL-1s to have found their way into a street-going 1969 Corvette. Mind you, this is pure speculation; no proof presently exists for any of these possibilities. According to Fred Frincke,

Press release artwork was actually produced for at least one of the "engines that never was for 1970." Shown here is the 460-horsepower LJ-2, the planned triple-carburetor 454. *Chevrolet Motor Division*

Chevrolet's Mk IV engine facility in Tonawanda, New York, built 154 ZL-1 427s, along with 549 L-88s. Tonawanda plant man and diehard big-block researcher Fran Preve claims a different score. His search through Chevrolet's official "Summary of Engines Shipped" papers uncovered 94 ZL-1s manufactured for Y-body Corvette applications: 80 for four-speeds, 14 for M40 automatics. Add to that another 90 all-aluminum 427s built for F-body ponycars by way of performance products manager Vince Piggins famed Central Office Production Order pipeline.

Along with the two recorded factory installations, one other ZL-1 big-block went into the Mako Shark II when it was restyled into the Manta Ray showcar in 1969. As for the remaining Corvette-coded crate engines . . . you tell us.

Sixty-nine ZL-1 Camaros rolled out of Chevrolet's backdoor in 1969 thanks to Piggins' clever use of GM's COPO loophole. Remember, before 1970 GM limited its intermediate and smaller lineups to no more than 400 ci of engine. Chevelles and Camaros could've been ordered with the 396 big-block but not the 427. Normally used for special fleet orders and such, the COPO request line proved to be a quick, easy way around corporate red tape. Piggins' end run resulted in the production of two different 427-powered Camaros in 1969. COPO number 9561 planted the Corvette's L-72 427 between ponycar flanks. COPO number 9560 referred to the ZL-1 Camaro. A third COPO code, number 9562, applied to the L-72 427 Chevelle.

According to longtime Chevrolet test engineer Bill Howell, Vince Piggins was the driving force behind the ZL-1 427's creation. It was Piggins who lobbied his bosses to fund an all-aluminum, big-block racing engine project in 1968, with the intention being to support, among others, Bruce McLaren's successful Canadian-American Challenge Cup team. Small-block Chevy-powered McLaren racing machines had begun their domination of the Can-Am series in 1967. Then Jim Hall had to go and "scratch-build" an aluminum big-block for his Chaparral race team—which was, of course, Chevy's unofficial research and development program. McLaren then threatened to look to Ford for a comparable lightweight big-block to power his 1968 Can-Am cars. Piggins

Strength in numbers for 1970— 300, 350, 370, 390, 460 hp.

Every Corvette is built tough right from the start. Our basic V8, the 300-hp Turbo-Fire 350, features a 10.25:1 compression ratio, a 4-barrel carb, cast aluminum alloy pistons and a precision-formed crank. With this, and all other Corvette engines, you get Corvette's dual exhausts with new rectangular outlets and Positraction rear axle standard.

Go one step up to the 350-hp Turbo-Fire 350, and you get an 11.0:1 compression ratio, impact-extruded aluminum alloy pistons, finned aluminum rocker covers, a high-performance cam and a forged steel alloy crank. Our 370-hp 350 features the same hardware as the 350-hp version plus an aluminum intake manifold, domed hood, special cam, special exhaust and mechanical lifters. Next step up. Our 390-

hp 454-cu.-in. Turbo-Jet V8. This engine uses a cast aluminum alloy intake manifold, chromed air cleaner and rocker covers and an extra-large oil pan. You also get a high-domed hood, heavier duty front stabilizer bar, heavier duty rear wheel spindle support arms, a rear suspension stabilizer bar, a larger capacity radiator, dual pulleys for

the fan and water pump and a higher performance starter motor.
Also available: our 460-hp Turbo-Jet 454 with a large 4-barrel carb, high-performance cam, mechanical lifters, aluminum cylinder heads and full-transistor ignition system.
Transmissions: standard gearbox is a floor-mounted, wide-range 4-Speed, 2.52:1 low gear. Also available, a 2.20:1 low (close ratio not available with 300-hp engine, wide range not available with 460-hp engine). With the 300-, 390- and 460-hp engines, you can order Turbo Hydra-matic. Just sit back and let this 3-range fully automatic transmission shift for itself; or upshift and downshift through the 1-2-3 quadrant yourself with all the benefits of a stick and none of the legwork.

Chevrolet Corvette Stingray Convertible with removable hardtop.   7

The original plan in 1970 was to pick up where the 427 left off with the 454 big-block. The L-88 427 would simply reappear as the LS-7 454. The fabled aluminum-head LS-7 almost made it into production— witness this page from the 1970 Corvette brochure. Other sources listed LS-7 output differently.

stepped in, promised Bruce his aluminum big-blocks, and the rest is racing history. Armed with the ZL-1, McLaren racers destroyed all Can-Am comers from 1968 to 1971, winning 32 of 37 events.

Once thoroughly baptized by fire on the 1968 Can-Am circuit, the ZL-1 427 then made its way in 1969 onto the Corvette's RPO list, as well as into Piggins' COPO delivery system. Although some references identified the ZL-1 V-8 as a "special L-88," creating the king of the 427s was by no means a simple matter of trading cast-iron for aluminum to make the cylinder block match those lightweight heads. While the ZL-1 and L-88 wore similar heads in 1969, the block was a truly unique piece of engineering.

Duntov turned to Fred Frincke for the expertise needed to fashion a high-performance engine completely out of aluminum. Casting was Frincke's forte; he knew his way around a foundry. Winters Foundry was responsible for casting the ZL-1's block, heads and intake.

Machining work and assembly was then completed at Tonawanda under a "100-percent parts inspection" policy in production areas that Duntov described as being "surgically clean." Ultimate precision was job one.

Frincke chose heat-treated 356 T-6 alloy for the block, which was cast with thickened walls and beefed-up main webs to compensate for the aluminum's weaker nature. Extra fortification also went into the block's deck to allow for the use of two extra cylinder head hold-down bolts. Head bolts were lengthened or screwed into steel Heli-Coil inserts to help further increase the grip between block and head. Trapped in the aluminum block's bores by the heads were eight cast-iron cylinder sleeves. Provisions for dry-sump oiling was also included in the block's design.

At the bottom end was a fully nitrided crank forged out of SAE 5140 steel and held in place, of course, by four-bolt main bearing caps. The same magnafluxed connecting rods introduced midyear in 1968 for the L-88 were used, they with their beefed 7/16-inch bolts, full-floating wrist pins, and Spiralock pin retainers.

ZL-1's heads—cast from 356 T-6 aluminum too—were based on the open-chamber units also introduced midway through 1968 for the L-88. Combustion chambers in those heads were opened up (thus the name) around the spark plug. Results of this change included a drop in compression (from 12.5:1 to 12:1) for the "Second-Design" L-88 because chamber volume increased from 106.8 cc to 118. Breathing, on the other hand, increased by a reported 30 percent thanks to the revised open chamber's closer relation to the exhaust port. Yet another benefit was lower emissions, which was really the goal of the open-chamber design. This achievement resulted from a 50 percent reduction in the quench or "squish" area, that is the space left over between the piston top and combustion chamber at top dead center.

Revised ports also contributed greatly to the open-chamber head's superior breathing. Although the large rectangular intake passages remained the same size as the first-generation L-88's, they were recontoured internally to help speed the air/fuel mixture into those open chambers. Exhaust ports were radically reshaped from rectangles into round passages to match up to the tube headers that would be quickly bolted up by the Speed Racer set in place of the mis-

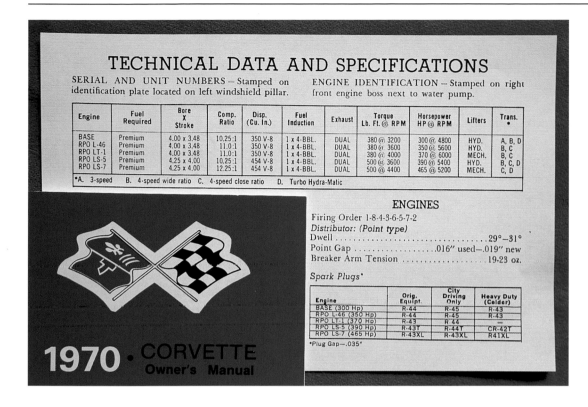

TECHNICAL DATA AND SPECIFICATIONS

SERIAL AND UNIT NUMBERS — Stamped on identification plate located on left windshield pillar.

ENGINE IDENTIFICATION — Stamped on right front engine boss next to water pump.

Engine	Fuel Required	Bore X Stroke	Comp. Ratio	Disp. (Cu. In.)	Fuel Induction	Exhaust	Torque Lb. Ft. @ RPM	Horsepower HP @ RPM	Lifters	Trans. •
BASE	Premium	4.00 x 3.48	10.25:1	350 V-8	1 x 4-BBL.	DUAL	380 @ 3200	300 @ 4800	HYD.	A, B, D
RPO L-46	Premium	4.00 x 3.48	11.0:1	350 V-8	1 x 4-BBL.	DUAL	380 @ 3600	350 @ 5600	HYD.	B, C
RPO LT-1	Premium	4.00 x 3.48	11.0:1	350 V-8	1 x 4-BBL.	DUAL	380 @ 4000	370 @ 6000	MECH.	B, C
RPO LS-5	Premium	4.25 x 4.00	10.25:1	454 V-8	1 x 4-BBL.	DUAL	500 @ 3600	390 @ 5400	HYD.	B, C, D
RPO LS-7	Premium	4.25 x 4.00	12.25:1	454 V-8	1 x 4-BBL.	DUAL	500 @ 4400	465 @ 5200	MECH.	C, D

•A. 3-speed   B. 4-speed wide ratio   C. 4-speed close ratio   D. Turbo Hydra-Matic

ENGINES

Firing Order 1-8-4-3-6-5-7-2
Distributor: (Point type)
Dwell ....29°–31°
Point Gap ....016" used—.019" new
Breaker Arm Tension ....19-23 oz.

Spark Plugs

Engine	Orig. Equipt.	City Driving Only	Heavy Duty (Colder)
BASE (300 Hp)	R-44	R-45	R-43
RPO L-46 (350 Hp)	R-44	R-45	R-43
RPO LT-1 (370 Hp)	R-43	R-44	—
RPO LS-5 (390 Hp)	R-43T	R-44T	CR-42T
RPO LS-7 (465 Hp)	R-43XL	R-43XL	R41XL

*Plug Gap—.035"

1970 • CORVETTE Owner's Manual

Another source to prematurely announce the LS-7 454's arrival in 1970 was the Corvette owner's manual. Notice the output figure listed—not even Chevrolet people knew exactly what was going on.

matched, rectangular-passage iron manifolds found on the factory-delivered ZL-1 Corvettes and Camaros.

Like the open-chamber L-88 head, the ZL-1 unit featured 2.19-inch intake valves and enlarged 1.88-inch exhausts. The ZL-1, however, was fitted with new TRW forged aluminum pistons with extra thick tops and strengthened pin bosses. These beefier slugs not only proved more durable than the L-88 units, they also reinstated the aluminum-head 427's original 12.5:1 compression by way of their increased dome area.

The ZL-1 427's solid-lifter cam was even more radical than the L-88's, at least as far as lift was concerned. Intake valve lift was 0.560-inch; exhaust was 0.600. Tom Langdon's tests, however, demonstrated that decreased durations cooperated better with those free-flowing, sewer-sized ports. The resulting shorter-duration cam, working in concert with the various reinforced internals, helped the ZL-1 wind out like no big-block on this planet. Seven-grand on the tach was no problem, and Chevrolet engineers claimed short bursts to 7,600 were within reason. Keeping the juices flowing during those high-rpm trips was the familiar 850-cfm Holley four-barrel.

All that carb, all that rev capability, all that cam, and Chevrolet once again insulted our intelligence with a bogus output rating. Maximum ZL-1 power was listed at 430 horses at 5,200 rpm. And once again everyone knew better. According to Tom Langdon, 525 horsepower was no problem for a ZL-1 right out of the crate. With "some attention to detail to the cylinder heads, etc.," producing up to 600 horsepower was within reason.

Perhaps Corvette buyers finally would have been treated to a larger dose of the truth had the L-88 and ZL-1 returned for 1970. They almost did. Duntov and crew fully intended on tweaking the enlarged 454-ci Mk IV big-block just as they had done with the 427. Early 1970 Corvette assembly manuals even announced this in print. The tri-carb LJ-2 454 would carry on in the best tradition of the L-71. The L-88 would be reborn as the LS-7 454. And the big-cube equivalent of the ZL-1 would be the LT-2. These 454s were all rated more realistically: The LJ-2 was listed at 460 horsepower; the LS-7 and LT-2 shared a 465-horse label.

Apparently the LJ-2 never made it much past the drawing board. Not so for the LT-2 454. "We built enough engines to test," explained Tom Langdon in 1999. "The aluminum-block LT-2 went into a showcar for a press review in 1970."

That review was actually held in the summer of 1969 to introduce 1970 models. But that

The LS-6 Chevelle Upstages the Corvette

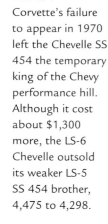

The LS-7 Corvette's failure to appear in 1970 left the Chevelle SS 454 the temporary king of the Chevy performance hill. Although it cost about $1,300 more, the LS-6 Chevelle outsold its weaker LS-5 SS 454 brother, 4,475 to 4,298.

The Corvette nearly always has been the favored son as far as Chevrolet Engineering was concerned. By the mid-1960s it was reigning supreme. When the fabulous Mk IV big-block was introduced in 1965, it was showcased in its most muscular form beneath a fiberglass hood. Those 396 cubic inches delivered 425 horsepower to a 1965 Corvette's overwhelmed rear rubber. In comparison, the new Malibu SS 396 introduced that year was fitted with a 375-horse version of the Mk IV V-8. Chevelles also were initially limited to no more than 400 cubes. The next year, Corvettes received an even bigger, badder Mk IV, the 427. And even after a GM upper office decree banned the use of multiple carburetor setups for its passenger-car lines, the 1967 Corvette rolled out with yet another even stronger big-block, the 435-horse L-71 427, fed by three Holley two-barrels. The tri-carb 427 remained the Corvette's most formidable street engine up through 1969.

Then came 1970, the year all hell broke loose in Detroit. As the new decade dawned, an escalating horsepower race reached its pinnacle. Runaway competition among the mighty musclecars then roaming the earth even inspired GM's sticks-in-the-mud to drop their 400-cid maximum displacement limit for their intermediate lineups. This then allowed Chevrolet to inadvertently upstage its performance flagship.

For the first time since the legendary 409s were running wild in the early 1960s, a car other than the Corvette stood as the most powerful Chevy on the street. Beyond that, the LS-6 SS 454 Chevelle emerged in 1970 wearing the highest advertised output rating of the entire musclecar era. Such numbers were often misleading back then, either overrated or underrated depending on which way the wind was blowing. But the 450-horsepower label assigned to the Chevelle's LS-6 454 V-8 was no paper tiger. That this rating then soared above all others advertised in 1970 was no coincidence. In many minds, the LS-6 Chevelle deserves the crown of king of the musclecars hands down.

Interestingly, Chevrolet engineers had almost labeled the hottest Corvette 427 in 1966 with a 450-horsepower decal. Cooler heads prevailed, however, and the actual label that did go to press read 425 horsepower. At that time all manufacturers had determined that a 425-horse rating represented the upper limit as far as tolerance was concerned—tolerance by government watchdogs who were already convinced that Detroit's horsepower race was running way out of control. But one year later Chevy engineers inched the Corvette's maximum-performance Corvette 427 to 435 horses. They then threw caution to the wind completely in 1970.

In truth the LS-6's record-setting output rating was undoubtedly a bit on the conservative side, but who was counting? Four-hundred-fifty ponies at 5,600 rpm represented more than enough giddyup power for even the heaviest leadfoot in 1970. Throw in a heaping helping of torque—a massive 500 ft-lb at 3,600 rpm—and melting the rubber to the rims was a foregone conclusion. On street tires with full exhausts the 1970 LS-6 Chevelles could scorch the quarter-mile in a tad more than 13 seconds. A few tweaks, open exhausts, and stickier treads dropped the car well into the 12-second class, a place not too many street cars have ever visited. Ever.

Arguments as to which machine actually won the musclecar era drag race will always persist, especially from the Hemi Mopar, Stage 1 Buick, and W-30 Olds camps. However, whenever the votes are counted it is always the LS-6 Chevelle that comes out on top. In 1970, critics knew even then that Chevrolet had made history. In the words of *Car Life's* road testers, the LS-6 454 was

Wearing iron cylinder heads (instead of aluminum) and squeezing fuel/air to a 11.25:1 ratio, the Chevelle's LS-6 454 produced 450 real horsepower. Notice the rare dual-snorkel air cleaner. Most LS-6 Chevelles probably featured the Cowl Induction hood and its rubber-sealed air cleaner. When a standard hood was chosen, the second favorite option was the open-element air cleaner.

"the best supercar engine ever released by General Motors." On the street, the 450-horse SS 454 demonstrated to many rivals that the LS-6 big-block was perhaps the best supercar engine ever released, period. "That's LS as in Land Speed Record," concluded *Motor Trend's* A.B. Sherman after watching an LS-6 Chevelle run from rest to 60 miles per hour in 6 seconds without even breaking a sweat.

Super Stock's staff went even further, comparing the LS-6 to the most powerful man-made force ever unleashed. "Driving a 450-horsepower Chevelle is like being the guy who's in charge of triggering atom bomb tests. You have the power, you know you have the power, and if you use the power bad things may happen. Things like arrest, prosecution, loss of license, broke to pieces, shredded tires, etc."

Like the atom bomb, the LS-6 Chevelle ended up being a doomsday weapon of sorts. It exploded on the scene in 1970 then quickly faded away into history. Even though magazine testers did get their hands on a 1971 LS-6 SS 454, actual production was cancelled as GM officials began closing the book on its musclecar legacy. Fortunately they saved the best for last.

And with the Chevelle SS lineup again relegated to mere mortal status, the Corvette resumed its rightful place atop Chevrolet's performance pecking order in 1971, this time with its own version of the LS-6 454 big-block.

showcar Langdon spoke of was the same 1969 Corvette that journalists had flogged the summer before. "That orange coupe was used in back-to-back press long-leads in 1968 and 1969," added Gib Hufstader. "In 1968 it was a ZL-1; in 1969 it was the LT-2." Again the coupe was equipped with a specially prepared Turbo Hydra-Matic, 4.88:1 gears, and drag slicks. And again most journalists didn't realize exactly what they were looking at beneath that lumpy ZL-2 hood.

"We learned that no one at the press day had bothered, or dared, ask what was actually in the car," explained a *Motor Trend* review of the mystery machine. Fortunately Langdon laid it all out for MT's staff. "The engine is a prototype for 1970," he said. "Let's just say [it's] very similar to a current ZL-1 all-aluminum unit. The aluminum cylinder heads are the same as currently released in the ZL-1, as is the camshaft, but this particular car has a special induction and exhaust system."

On top was a truly enormous Holley four-barrel that flowed somewhere between 1,200 to 1,400 cubic feet per minute. At the other end of the process was a set of custom-built 180-degree headers. Looking like something right off a race track, these exhausts matched two pairs of cylinders from opposite banks together into huge collectors to take advantage of the engine's natural firing order pulses. According to Hufstader, these tangled-up tubes freed up about a dozen more horsepower compared to conventional headers. There was also another more noticeable result. "Those 180-degree headers gave the LT-2 a ripping sound," said Hufstader.

Like its ZL-1 427 forerunner, the LT-2 454 eclipsed the quarter-mile in 11 seconds flat with ease. And with anyone at the wheel. According to *Motor Trend*, the best pass was 10.60 seconds at 132 miles pr hour. But the best was also the last.

The all-aluminum 454 was never seen again after its press showing in 1969. According to Hufstader, the LT-2 engine was homologated for competition but was axed well before it got anywhere near the Corvette's official options list for 1970. Times were changing and so were attitudes at GM involving performance—or in the Corvette's case, excessive performance. Corporate killjoys no longer wanted to waste good money on pure flights of fancy. The days of selling race cars on the street were all but over anyway thanks to growing

One year after Corvette buyers were teased with the LS-7, the LS-6 454 emerged to revive their faith in Zora Duntov's engineering team. Though tamed by lowered compression, the 1971 Corvette's LS-6 V-8 still rated at 425 horsepower. LS-6 Corvette production was only 188.

safety concerns, ever-tightening emissions standards and wallet-wilting insurance costs.

Of the exotic 454 big-blocks initially mentioned in early plans for 1970 production, the aluminum-head LS-7 came closest to reality. It was not only listed in assembly manuals and AMA spec sheets, it also made it into 1970 factory brochures and owner's manuals, although some confusion existed as to what reality really was. Mundane black-and-white engineering papers and the pretty color brochures listed compression at 11.25:1 and output at 460 horsepower. Like the early assembly manuals, the 1970 owner's manual claimed 465 horsepower, as well as 12.25:1 compression. Solid lifters were a given.

An LS-7 Corvette also made it into the magazine road test arena in 1970, where again a 465-horsepower rating was quoted. Duntov and Hufstader unveiled the aluminum-head 454 at southern California's Riverside Raceway in December 1969. Eric Dahlquist drove the car that day but didn't report any performance times in his March 1970 *Motor Trend* review.

What he did mention was the LS-7's new dual-disc clutch, yet another trick piece transferred

from the racetrack to the street. Hufstader today is still proud of this unit, which could handle every pound of big-block torque yet required far less pedal effort than Chevrolet's typical heavy-duty clamper. Doubling the friction area by using two 10-inch clutch discs meant a lower-tension pressure plate could be incorporated. "No one, or nearly no one at the preview missed a shift," claimed Dahlquist. "The harder and faster you went, the better it seemed to work—all day long."

After the day's work was done, it was Paul Van Valkenburgh's turn to drive. And drive. And drive. He picked up the LS-7 coupe at Riverside and returned it to Detroit, recounting his wild 2,500-mile ride in *Sports Car Graphic*'s March 1970 issue. "What's it like to drive a loaded 454-ci Stingray?" he asked. "It's like taxiing a DC3 at full throttle up and down a freshly plowed runway. At least that's what it rides and sounds like." From there, Van Valkenburgh's recount apparently contradicted reality a time or two. According to him, the LS-7 featured a hydraulic cam and 11:1 compression. Go figure.

At least he did crunch some speed numbers. "We easily turned a quarter-mile in 13.8

The aluminum-head LS-6 454 received full emissions controls and a timid compression ratio of 9:1, yet it still could burn up the quarter-mile in the 13-second range. It was offered in the Corvette for 1971 only.

seconds and 108 miles per hour—with full fuel, passenger, and luggage for two." And full exhausts, standard Firestone Wide Ovals, smog pump, radio, heater, and so on. And a fan shroud. Unlike the L-88, the LS-7 was set up for street duty. The car itself also featured a conventional, nonfunctional big-block hood, which meant the aluminum-head 454 was fitted with a low-rise intake manifold instead of the high-riser used by the L-88, ZL-1, and LT-2.

Like Dahlquist, Van Valkenburgh loved that clutch. "The roughness of double-disc clutches has been disproven by Chevrolet, as their version is so light and smooth that it precipitates speed shifts—because you can get the clutch pedal down and up before you can get the accelerator up and down." On the other hand (foot?) he wasn't particularly fond of feeding this beast. "A desirable accessory with the 454 LS-7 engine would be a reliable co-pilot to watch the fuel gauge sink and keep feeding cruising range data to the driver between gas stations."

Single-digit fuel "economy" aside, Van Valkenburgh claimed the LS-7 Corvette represented one of the world's best sports car buys as far as "performance-per-dollar" was concerned. He felt all that "awesome power" was definitely worth the price, which he quoted at "well over

seven grand." "We close with the old Texas proverb," he concluded. "'If you care who's quickest, don't get caught shoveling manure behind someone else's 465 horses.'"

Whether or not the LS-7 could have put the Corvette up on a higher plateau became a moot point once Chevrolet cancelled the advertised option before it could go from paper to plastic. Coupled with GM efforts to tone down its "hot car" image in 1970 were Chevy officials' moves to cut back on costly options that complicated assembly lines. "De-pro" was the company jargon for this de-proliferation program. One de-pro victim was the 350-horsepower L-46 small-block, deleted after 1970. Another was the LS-7. Both losses disappointed Duntov, but at least one other engineer didn't exactly feel the same way concerning the latter cancellation.

"I was opposed to the LS-7, but I was so low down the totem pole it had no effect," said Tom Langdon. "The L-88 already had demonstrated substantial durability problems. A longer stroke inherently creates more problems through increased friction. Increasing the stroke to go from 427 ci to 454 only aggravated the [L-88's] problems. We hadn't even solved the 427's problems yet and we were making [them] worse."

Langdon also didn't agree with another old Texas proverb, the one that claimed that there was no substitute for cubic inches. He felt that in this case there was no need to jump from 427 ci to 454. "Increasing the stroke without enlarging the bore doesn't necessarily translate into a real increase in power," he said. "Some of that extra power is eaten up by increased friction. A good 427 [L-88] would put out about 600 horsepower. The 454 pulled more torque, but power was just about the same as the L-88." Yet another moot point.

By all accounts the 1970 LS-7 Corvette that Dahlquist and Van Valkenburgh drove was the only one built—at least for public exposure. According to research through Tonawanda paperwork, the New York plant shipped seven LS-7 454s to St. Louis, and five of those were returned. Terry McManmon, the National Corvette Restorers Society 1970–72 technical advisor, claims differently. He says Tonawanda officials told him that maybe two to four LS-7 engines were built and all were sent to Chevrolet Engineering in Warren, Michigan, for testing and prototype installations. Another LS-7 mule or two was probably created, but all were dismantled by order. Or were they?

"I asked Zora a few years back about the possibility of an LS-7 Corvette surviving," said McManmon in March 1999. "He told me with a wry smile that he personally signed the order to destroy the LS-7 test cars. But the way he smiled, I wondered if he was giving me the real story."

As for the one known LS-7 Corvette, it was dismantled. Then, according to Gib Hufstader, its aluminum-head 454 was stolen a few years later out of Chevy Engineering's back lot. "I never lost the stuff I tried to hide," said Hufstader, "but this one got away. It was about 1973 or 1975. A couple guys apparently jumped the fence one night and we never saw it again."

With the LS-7 now a soon-to-be-forgotten footnote in the Corvette history books, Duntov's engineers were left with little to show in 1970 for all their fast thinking. The exciting, new LT-1 small-block did debut in 1970. But in the big-block ranks the lukewarm 390-horse LS-5 454 was as hot as it got—beneath Corvette hoods, that is. The LS-7's early demise also left America's only sports car in a unique position: second fiddle. Not only was the 1970 big-block Corvette no longer this country's most

powerful performance machine, it wasn't even the most powerful Chevy.

That title was claimed by the LS-6 SS 454 Chevelle, arguably the king of the musclecar era. "The LS-6 was our big success," claimed Hufstader. Wearing cast-iron closed-chamber heads, the original LS-6 454 was rated at 450 industry-leading horses beneath A-body hoods in 1970. Compression was 11.25:1. Although early 1970 paperwork listed RPO LS-6 as an option for both the Chevelle and Camaro Super Sports, that latter combo never arrived—yet another de-pro perhaps?

Oddly, an LS-6 Corvette never showed up in 1970 either. Some, including Tom Langdon, have since claimed that the 450-horsepower 454 didn't become a Corvette option that first year because Chevrolet didn't have a suitable low-rise intake manifold available for the LS-6/Y-body application. Yet it did for the LS-7? Okay, so perhaps flow characteristic differences between the aluminum open-chamber heads and the iron closed-chamber units may have precluded a simple technology swap-out. Maybe, maybe not. There was no problem fitting the LS-5 454 with a hood-clearing intake in 1970.

A better explanation for the situation probably involved Chevrolet's planned pecking order. Even though early paperwork also had the 1970 Chevelle SS getting its own LS-7, the 465-horsepower Corvette would've still claimed no less than a tie for Chevrolet's top power spot in 1970. Planners apparently never even considered an LS-6 option for the 1970 Corvette with the LS-7 deal all but inked. Mention of an LS-7 Chevelle option then quickly evaporated, leaving the promised LS-7 Corvette to roll on toward Chevrolet's late-starting 1970 production run with intentions of once again standing alone atop the division's performance pyramid. According to Gib Hufstader, once the LS-7 454 was cancelled, it was far too late to call up the LS-6 as a stand-in. The waters were muddied even further the following year when Corvette buyers were offered RPO LS-6, but Chevelle customers weren't—this after magazines road tested a 1971 LS-6 SS 454. De-pro again?

"De-comp" might also have been an appropriate catch-phrase for the Corvette's LS-6. Like all GM engines in 1971, it experienced a compression cut, in this case to 9:1. This, in turn, resulted in a corresponding drop in horsepower, from 450 to 425. On the positive side were the aluminum open-chamber cylinder heads bolted on in place of the Chevelle's iron heads. Much of the rest of the 1971 LS-6's makeup also mimicked the L-88. Valve sizes were 2.19 inches intake, 1.88 exhaust. The iron block featured four-bolt mains. Rods were forged steel with big 7/16-inch bolts. Although their dome heights were much shorter than those found in L-88s, the low-compression LS-6 pistons were again TRW forged aluminum pieces.

On top, a 780-cubic-feet-per-minute Holley four-barrel sat on a low-rise, dual-plane intake cast of aluminum. The solid-lifter cam bumped up both valves by 0.519 inch through 1.7:1 stamped steel rockers. Duration was 316 degrees on the intake side, 302 on the exhaust. Ignition was transistorized. Available transmissions were listed as the M21 close-ratio four-speed, M22 Rock Crusher, and M40 Turbo Hydra-Matic. The clutch was the excellent dual-disc unit demonstrated behind the LS-7 in 1970.

Price for RPO LS-6 in 1971 also continued in the best tradition of the L-88. At $1,220, it was little wonder only 188 customers checked off the aluminum-head 454 option that year, leaving the main man disappointed yet again. "It's Duntov's favorite engine and he's tortured because few customers can afford it," claimed a *Car and Driver* report. But this time Zora's letdown may have been self-inflicted. "Maybe for street engine I make mistake," he admitted to *Car and Driver.* "Aluminum heads are expensive and that weight doesn't matter on the street."

Even more expensive was RPO ZR-2, the Special Purpose Turbo-Jet 454 option. Originally mentioned for the stillborn LS-7 in 1970, the ZR-2 equipment group mirrored the ZR-1 racing package offered for the LT-1 small-block from 1970 to 1972 (see chapter 4). Along with the LS-6 454, RPO ZR-2 included F41 heavy-duty suspension, J50/J56 power-assisted heavy-duty brakes, and the L-88's Harrison radiator—without a fan shroud, of course. All comforts and conveniences, including radio and air conditioning, were not available. No way, no how. The only transmission choice was the brutal Rock Crusher.

Equally brutal was that suspension. The seven-leaf spring in back was nearly twice as stout as the standard unit. Front coils were 75 percent stronger. Obviously the ZR-2 was not for soft-tailed drivers. Nor was it for the weak of wallet. The bottom line for RPO ZR-2 was

$1,747. A mere 12 were sold in 1971, hopefully to racers only.

On the street, the "standard" LS-6 Corvette did not disappoint those with memories of the L-89 427 still fresh in their minds. *Car and Driver*'s road test of a 1971 LS-6 backed up by that dreaded 3.36:1 economy axle still resulted in a 13.8/104.65 time slip. Zero to 60 equaled 5.3 seconds. As usual, more speed was just an option check-off and turn of the wrench away.

"The LS-6 will definitely produce better times with a higher numerical axle ratio and with a freer exhaust system," read *Car and Driver*'s conclusions. "According to Duntov, 50 horsepower is lost in the mufflers. That, however, is life. You have to have mufflers on the street. California laws say they have to be quiet ones and the LS-6's are—stifled even. The pulses are still distinct but they're muted. Giants in padded cells."

Car Craft's editors made every effort to free those giants. They added headers, sidepipes, 4.56:1 gears, and slicks. Although they expected better, their best test run still produced an E.T. of 12.64 seconds at 114.21 miles per hour. Not long after this sizzling pass, one of *Car Craft*'s less experienced leadfoots put a couple of the LS-6's rods through its oil pan—somewhat of a fitting exclamation point for a story entitled "Goodbye Forever LS-6." *Car Craft*'s crew knew even as they were flogging one of the strongest Corvettes ever built that they would probably never see such speed again from America's only sports car. They were well aware of the fact that the LS-6 was the "last of the fast Corvettes." Chevrolet had already made it clear that the option wouldn't return for 1972.

De-proliferation took on an entirely new meaning after 1971. Certain extra-high-performance Corvette options were de-pro victims before that year. Afterward, it was horsepower in general that felt the axe. At least before that happened Chevrolet was able to let loose the hot-to-trot legends labeled L-88, ZL-1, and LS-6. They didn't call these production engines big-blocks for nothing. These rats apologized to no one for their rude, raucous, high-revving natures. Sure, Mk IV rat motors would remain a Corvette option up through 1974. But the story just wasn't the same after the LS-6 was cancelled. It truly was, as *Car Craft* announced, the "end of an era."

Never again would the Corvette faithful live so large.

Chapter 4

THE MOUSE THAT ROARED
LT-1 Corvettes, 1970–72

Purists have long scoffed at the notion that the Corvette is a sports car. A true sports car. *Car and Driver*'s ever-caustic Brock Yates may have put it best, from a naysayer's perspective, in 1974 when he claimed that "the Corvette is the Frank Sinatra of sports cars—a hoofer with a gooey frosting of 'stardom' concealing rather limited artistry." He didn't stop there, calling Chevrolet's two-seater "a manifestation of a brand of mass-class, chrome-and-plastic elegance embodied elsewhere in Playboy Clubs, Las Vegas, double-knit suits, diamond pinkie rings, Master Charge cards, Ramada Inns and speedboats with curved windshields." Corvette lovers who still mourn Old Blue Eyes, are lifetime *Playboy* subscribers, jet off to Vegas regularly, and so on, can still find Yates at *Car and Driver*, 2002 Hogback Road, Ann Arbor, Michigan 48105.

More to the point, or at least more to the point being pushed here, were Yates' 1974 comments concerning the Corvette's competition record, which he considered "a compendium of the inconsequential." He pooh-poohed "those endless SCCA amateur championships, where the only time they didn't beat each other, Corvettes were trounced by [Carroll Shelby's] Cobras." And he dismissed "the class structures of international racing [that] make it impossible for Corvettes to compete for overall wins against the lighter European prototypes" as a poor excuse. According to him, "it [still] does dampen national chauvinism to witness those big, red-white-and-blue 454-ci thumpers getting gobbled up by various little rockets from Europe race after race after race." Concluded

Yates, "the marque has been on the automotive scene for over 20 years, solidly entrenched as one of the fastest automobiles in the world, yet it has not won a single major motor race! Aside from a couple of victories by John Greenwood in the badly weakened 1973 Trans-Am series and some class wins in endurance competition, Corvettes have been smoked off by everything from Porsches and Ferraris to its factory sister—the Camaro—so often that I view the machine as a bad joke when dressed up in racing numbers."

Again, send your cards or letters to *Car and Driver*, not this author.

Although Yates' opinions may have hit a bit hard, or a lot hard depending on where you sit, they did arrive quite close to home. Being an American car born of American sensibilities helped make the Corvette its own worst enemy—as far as its sports car status was concerned—for many years. From the beginning, it has always been too big, too heavy, too powerful, even too comfortable and convenient. Sports cars, at least from a world view, were meant to be much more nimble, if not spritely. So what if a Corvette can beat a Porsche or Jag from point A to B in the shortest distance? Straight lines are harder to find across the Atlantic where the sports car was born and refined. Germans, Italians, and the British have long built true sport cars: lightweight, sure-footed machines able to jaunt about through twists and turns with nary a care. Americans, on the other hand, have rarely built anything other than land yachts: big cars with big engines that spit out, among other things, horsepower by the barrel.

That hood may not have been functional, but that didn't stop the LT-1 small-block from pumping out power like a big-block. Rivals in 1970 who didn't know what that little decal meant had another thing coming.

LT-1 Corvette production, coupes and convertibles, was 1,287 in 1970. Another 1,949 followed in 1971. It cost $447 to drop Chevy's hottest small-block 350 into a Corvette engine bay in 1970.

Big-valve heads, a solid-lifter cam and 11:1 compression helped the LT-1 350 produced 370 horsepower in 1970. Air conditioning was not available with the LT-1 in 1970 and 1971.

A wimp in the minds of the typical American horsepower hound, the first Corvette's Blue Flame Six was still a major hunk of macho iron in comparison to nearly all European sports car powerplants of the day, many of which relied on two less cylinders. Then Ed Cole and the gang dropped a V-8 beneath that forward-hinged hood in 1955. Again small by U.S. standards, Chevrolet's ground-breaking 265 small-block nonetheless appeared more like a monstrosity to ascot-wearing drivers in their Guliettas, MGAs, 356 Porsches, and the like. They had another thing coming 10 years later when the brutish 396 big-block was shoehorned between the 1965 Sting Ray's fiberglass flanks. Although it didn't necessarily add any additional weight into the equation, the appearance of the enlarged 454 big-block in 1970 did nothing to dissuade beliefs that the Corvette was an overpowered, overburdened beast.

Thus was created the Catch-22 that taunted Zora Duntov throughout his two decades at GM. More horsepower was the key to keeping the Corvette alive beyond 1955, but more power meant more cubic inches, and more cubes meant more engine. More engine, of course, meant more weight; not only more total pounds on the scales, but more unwanted pounds up front over the front wheels.

Don't be fooled, though. Duntov may have tried his darndest to build a better-balanced Corvette with a lighter, yet still strong engine mounted amidships. But that didn't mean he was morally opposed to big-block brute force. On the contrary—he loved the 427. And while his greatest disappointment came when GM finally squelched his midengine idea, he later also expressed dismay that Chevrolet failed to release the all-aluminum LS-7 454 in 1970.

Zora could be both a dreamer and a realist. He was no fool; he fully recognized the budgetary realities at GM, as well as the need to keep the Corvette out in front as America's top-performing automobile. As a 1969 *Car Life* report explained, "We asked Duntov if he had considered a 2,000-lb., 300-bhp Corvette." His reply? "He has, and the closest he's been able to come is a 3,500-lb., 435-bhp Corvette."

Again, class, repeat after me: All that weight required all that power, all that power required all that engine, and all that engine precluded cutting down all that weight.

Being bigger and heavier overall compared to overseas rivals was only the beginning as far as the Corvette's handicap on the international sports car stage was concerned. Superior handling, not supreme horsepower, long has been the top priority among the world-class sporting crowd. Corvette handling, while superior by American perspectives, fell even further behind world-class standards as the car grew heavier by the nose. Until recent years, Corvette owners attempting foreign relations on long and winding roads were more often than not embarrassed by drivers spurring on far fewer horses let loose by much less engine displacement.

Suitable solutions to the problem never did fit within the high-volume, profit-intensive production parameters that were, are, and always will be among the facts of life in Detroit. Although the Corvette has continually stretched the limits at General Motors, job one has always been to keep costs in line at all costs. Duntov's midengine dream machine never made it much beyond the drawing board in the 1970s because such a design would have raised the Corvette's price who knows how far beyond what the market would bear. But while relocating the engine never happened, moving the transmission to the rear did, albeit a quarter century later. Today's C5 is, accordingly, the best balanced Corvette ever, as well as the Corvette best suited to do battle with foreign invaders.

The Corvette most able to represent this country on the world sports car stage 30 years ago wasn't the outrageous L-88 or its more streetable 435-horse cousin. Not even close. Granted, big-block Sharks were among some of the quickest machines ever built. Off the line. But once faced with vectoring left or right again and again they could've easily ended up off the

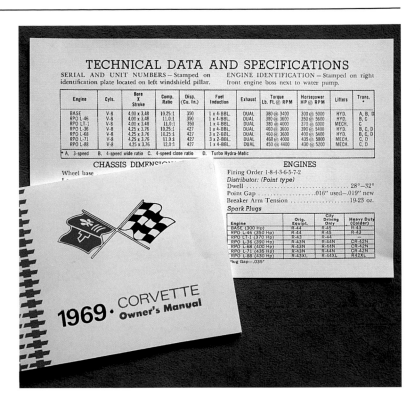

road. The so-called "rat-motored" Vettes, the 427s and 454s, were best suited for stoplight-to-stoplight competition here at home with red-white-and-blue-blooded musclecars like Hemi Mopars and Cobra Jet Mustangs.

The Corvette Duntov undoubtedly would have been more willing to drive in Europe then was the legendary LT-1, introduced in 1970. Built in small numbers up through 1972, the LT-1 probably represented the closest the C3 Corvette came to garnering true respect as a world-class sports car. *Car Life's* editors in August 1970 called it "the best of all possible Corvettes." "Forget the LS-7," they continued. "Don't wait for the mid-engine prototype. The LT-1 is here, and it's ready." Earlier that summer, *Motor Trend's* Chuck Koch concluded that the LT-1 was "much closer to its German competitor than most Porsche owners care to admit." According to *Sports Car Graphic's* Paul Van Valkenburgh, the 1970 LT-1 was "better in most ways than every Italian/British/German two-seat street GT available at thrice the price."

In 1971 *Motor Trend's* Eric Dahlquist was also quick to point out how well the LT-1 stacked up dollar for dollar against its much more expensive European rivals. "We were almost embarrassed to find that despite Detroit's

One year before Chevrolet officially announced the LS-7 option then never coughed it up, the paperwork guys were again leaping before they looked. Plans to introduce the LT-1 350 in 1969 fell through, but not before the 1969 Corvette owner's manuals were printed.

Comparisons between the Corvette and purported rivals—even dating back to the fiberglass two-seater's earliest days—have never really panned out. Ford's original Thunderbird was a bird of another feather entirely. Studebaker's supercharged Avanti was close but no cigar. Carroll Shelby's Cobras could run, but they couldn't hide their totally uncivilized nature. Shelby's Mustangs, GT 350 or GT 500, had their own niche. American Motors' two-seat AMX was here and gone before anyone really noticed. Pantera? DeLorean? Bricklin? Not a chance. No matter how fast, no matter how sexy, no other car has ever been able to capture the imagination, to stir the souls of both men and women like Chevrolet's 'glass-bodied baby.

But if there was one machine that did a damned good Corvette impersonation it was another Chevy. The Camaro, introduced in 1967 to do battle with Ford's wildly popular Mustang, offered its fair share of performance potential. It was relatively lightweight and could become quite nimble with the right options. It could get downright fast too, with a 396-ci big-block beneath that long hood.

Big-block power, however, compromised handling. The supreme Camaro as far as fully balanced, sports car-type performance was concerned was the famed Z/28, also introduced in 1967. The Z/28's hot, high-winding 302 small-block V-8, coupled with a race-ready chassis, helped turn more than one Corvette crazy's head, especially so if that particular crazy was a few grand short of his dream of living life in the fiberglass fast lane.

Today's horsepower hounds know the concept as "the biggest bang for the buck." There was no doubt that the baddest big-block Corvettes of the late-1960s offered the best bang, but at what cost? Just as there has always been no substitute for cubic inches, there is also nothing stronger than the power of cold, hard cash. How fast you want to go always has and always will depend on how much you have to spend.

By 1970, the Corvette's base price had surpassed the $5,000 plateau for the first time, and for this amount a buyer only received the standard 300-horse 350 small-block. Installing the 454 big-block added another $289 to the bottom line, opting for the 370-horsepower LT-1 small-block upped the ante by nearly 450 bucks.

The original Z/28 package in the late 1960s cost a few dollars more than the Corvette's LT-1 engine option did in 1970. But for about $460, Camaro buyers not only got their own exclusive V-8—the 290-horsepower 302—they also went home with a trick suspension, 15x7 wheels, a nice dose of exterior imagery, and a heavy-duty cooling system. Although other mandatory heavy-duty options (four-speed manual, front disc brakes) did raise the Z/28's price further, a Camaro coupe's base sticker in 1969 was still only a tad more than $2,700.

You get the picture, no? Fifty-five hundred dollars was a lot of dough 30 years ago. Thirty-five hundred was a pile then too, but it wasn't $5,500. All things being relative, the first-generation Z/28 Camaro indeed qualified as a "poorman's Corvette." While the prestige obviously wasn't quite the same, much of the performance was, and it came at a price many considered affordable.

Then along came the second-generation Z/28. You would have to search far and wide to find a car that compared as favorably, as closely, with the Corvette as the 1970 1/2 Z/28 Camaro. Again, its well-balanced performance was a given. But this time around its image took a major turn toward the Corvette's stratosphere thanks to a sexy restyle that most critics couldn't resist. GM's all new F-body shell, introduced in February 1970 (thus the 1970 1/2 designation), created newfound excitement for both Camaro and Firebird buyers. From nose to tail, from top to bottom, this curvaceous, thoroughly modern body represented the biggest styling hit of the new decade. "It's quiet, quick, beautiful and all the parts look and act as though they belong together," claimed *Sports Car Graphic's* Paul Van Valkenburgh in reference to the 1970 1/2 Z/28.

Beauty beneath that bodacious skin included a new powerplant too. The standard small-block for the next-generation Z/28 was the LT-1 350, the same LT-1 as the Corvette's with one exception: The Z/28's LT-1 was advertised at 10 fewer horsepower. Ten horses on paper mattered little, though. More than 1 horsepower per cubic inch was still more than 1 horsepower per cubic inch, and 360 horses were more than enough to move the Z/28 into a higher class of performance. With a much wider, more useful power band compared to the 302, the 350 LT-1 offered an instantaneous brand of throttle response that earlier Z/28 drivers could only imagine.

According to *Car Life's* testers, "the [new] Z/28 is as close to a mild-mannered racing car as the industry has come.

Beneath a Camaro's hood, the LT-1 350 was rated at 360 horsepower, 10 less than its Corvette cousin. No matter how you sliced it, though, this ponycar was hot to trot.

As it has in recent years, talk in the early 1970s had Chevrolet combining the Camaro and Corvette into a more affordable, yet still sporty package. Camaro owners in 1970 almost didn't have to wait for that rumor to become reality. The sexy 1970 1/2 Z28 offered every bit as much performance as the hottest small-block Corvette did that year. Both shared the LT-1 350 V-8—the Corvette as an option, the Camaro as standard power.

Despite the added weight and tougher emissions controls, it's faster than ever, and in a way that makes the car driveable by anybody." That included drivers familiar with Corvette-style performance.

Van Valkenburgh's *SCG* test of the 1970 1/2 Z/28 was a comparison report that pitted the new Camaro against a 1970 LT-1 Corvette. His conclusion came right off the bat in his headline: "They really are all the same in the dark!" In all tests—acceleration, braking, lateral g, and so on—the two ran neck and neck, with the Z/28 actually slightly outscoring the Corvette a time or two. Zero to 60 times were 6.7 seconds for the Corvette, 6.5 for the Camaro.

The only area where the Corvette showed off a noticeable advantage was aerodynamics, but that was expected. On the flipside, the Z/28's advantage was even more noticeable, as well as more meaningful to Average Joe. The as-tested price tags for the two heavily optioned Chevrolets in *SCG's* comparo read $6,357 for the Corvette, $4,690 for the Z/28. Had the Camaro in question not included the RS equipment and a few other optional diddies, the price differential between the two machismo mills would have been every bit of $2,000. Concerning this figure, Van Valkenburgh could only restate the obvious. "Think of the non-automotive things you can spend $2,000 on," he wrote. "If you choose the Vette, you're spending it on something that doesn't even exist—your image."

Haughty Corvette owners in 1970 could look down from above and snicker all they wanted. But it was the Z/28 guys that got the last laugh—and this one lasted all the way to the bank.

myopia and failures they can still build one of the best cars anywhere, not for nine or ten grand, but six," he wrote in praise of the biggest, baddest small-block Corvette to date. The expensive European that Dahlquist used for a measuring stick against the LT-1 was Britain's V-12 E-type Jag. "The Corvette is a better car," he boldly, if not bravely, concluded.

The LT-1 earned such accolades by combining rat-like muscle with the nimbleness inherent in Corvettes fitted with the venerable V-8 affectionately known by Chevy-heads as the "mouse motor." With midengined possibilities representing more fantasy than fact, the best a bias-conscious buyer could do in the early 1970s was stick with the 350-cid small-block, which weighed about 150 pounds less than the Mk IV big-block. This, in turn, meant a 350-powered 1970 Stingray achieved a more preferable 50/50 front/rear weight balance, making it more of a treat to drive through the twisties compared to the nose-heavy 454 Corvette. This and the LT-1 brand of 350 V-8 injected 370 horses into the mix.

It had been five years since Corvette buyers had seen a small-block as powerful as the LT-1 350, and its debut instantly invited comparisons to earlier milestones. According to *Car and Driver*, any other power source was "of little interest to the Corvette purist, the man who remembers the soul and vitality of the high-winding fuel-injected 283 when it was the only street engine in the country that put out one horsepower per cubic inch. Today's equivalent is the LT-1."

Like so many other publications over the last 40-something years, *Car and Driver* didn't exactly get the facts right. The Chrysler 300B's optional 354-cid Hemi V-8 was advertising 355 horsepower in 1956, but who was counting, right? As it was, the 283-horse 283 "fuelie" introduced one year later was only the beginning. Top fuel-injected output grew to 290 horses in 1958, 315 in 1961. It hit 360 horsepower when small-block displacement expanded to 327 ci in 1962. By 1964, the injected L-84 327 was producing 375 horsepower. Then along came those big-block bullies the following year, which was the last for the L-84.

Prior to 1970, the hottest noninjected small-block ever cooked up was the L-76 327 of 1964–65. Essentially an L-84 with a four-barrel in place of the Rochester F.I. unit, the solid-lifter L-76 was rated at 365 horsepower. It too

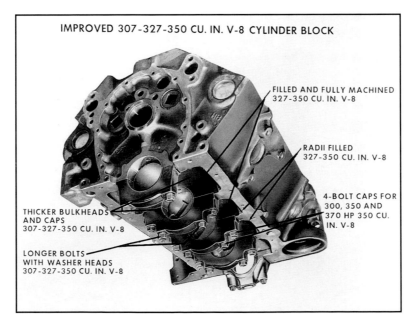

IMPROVED 307-327-350 CU. IN. V-8 CYLINDER BLOCK

FILLED AND FULLY MACHINED
327-350 CU. IN. V-8

RADII FILLED
327-350 CU. IN. V-8

4-BOLT CAPS FOR
300, 350 AND
370 HP 350 CU.
IN. V-8

THICKER BULKHEADS
AND CAPS
307-327-350 CU. IN. V-8

LONGER BOLTS
WITH WASHER HEADS
307-327-350 CU. IN. V-8

Chevrolet's vaunted small-block legacy began in 1955 with this 265-ci V-8. A short stroke and lightweight valve gear featuring stamped steel ball-stud rocker arms made this all-new, thoroughly modern overhead-valve V-8 rev like nobody's business. *Chevrolet Public Relations*

The performance mouse-motor's cylinder block was already one beefy piece even before engineers began building the LT-1 350. *Chevrolet Motor Division*

was discontinued after 1965. The LT-1's debut in 1970 represented both the arrival of a new king of the carbureted mouse motor hill and a return of mechanical tappets to the small-block Corvette lineup.

The 370-horse LT-1 350 also was essentially an enlarged variation of yet another hot solid-lifter Chevy small-block, although saying that begged the question of which came first, chicken or egg? As a June 1971 *Car and Driver* report explained it, the LT-1 "is probably even better known as the Z28, which is what it is

called when ordered in the Camaro. Corvette engineers originated the idea so Duntov winces when you say the two engines are the same, but they are."

A second LT-1, this one rated at 360 horsepower, served as the heart and soul for the new Z/28 Camaro introduced early in 1970. Previous Z/28s used the hotter-than-hell 302 small-block hybrid, and it was this engine that the LT-1 was based on. The 290-horsepower 302 was created exclusively for the original Trans-Am Camaro in 1967 by stuffing a 283 crank into a 327 block. A huge 800-cubic feet per minute Holley four-barrel, a loping solid-lifter cam, and big-valve heads helped make the Z/28 302 "a happy and extremely potent screamer," according to *Sports Car Graphic's* Jerry Titus.

Creating the LT-1 V-8 was simply logical. Knowing that there usually is no substitute for cubic inches, Chevy engineers couldn't help but recognize the obvious. All things being equal, more displacement almost always means more power potential. And by most counts 350 amounted to more than 302. If the Z/28's happy little small-block was such a potent screamer, imagine what 48 more cubes might do for this mighty mouse. So many pieces in Chevy's small-block parts bins mixed and matched so easily, working that Z/28 magic on the 350 V-8 was simply a matter of turning a wrench.

Too bad those bins weren't bottomless.

After serving two years beneath Camaro hoods, the 350-cid small-block finally replaced the venerable 327 V-8 as the Corvette's standard power source in 1969. Initially spec'ed out that year was the base 300-horsepower 350, the 350-horse L-46 350, and the LT-1. That's right, the LT-1. In 1969. Early factory paperwork listed the engine that year, and more than one press source applauded its arrival. "If you're hung up on a Stingray and you want one that handles as well as it hauls, check out the new 370-horsepower LT-1 350-cuber; it's the only way to go," announced a headline in the May

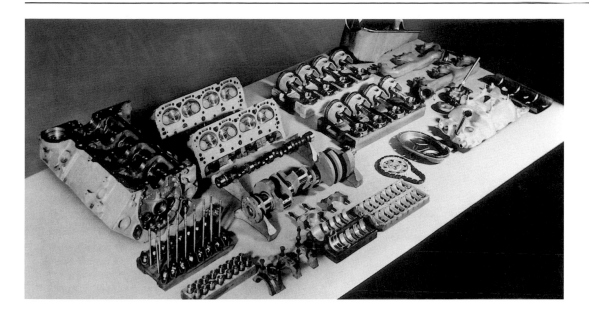

The LT-1's forefather was the first Z/28 Camaro's exclusive powerplant, the 290-horsepower 302. This engine was created specially to legalize the Z/28 Camaro for SCCA Trans-Am racing. It was destroked down within the SCCA's 305-ci limit by inserting a 283 crank into a 327 block. *Chevrolet Motor Division*

1969 issue of *Cars* magazine. "Besides being a super-duty engine with high-rpm potential, it's also relatively light," continued the review a few lines below. "This factor plus its high torque rating makes for a dynamite handling and accelerating package."

Such announcements, however, proved premature as the LT-1 never became a production Corvette in 1969, although one such car apparently was sold. As a July 1969 *Car Life* report explained, "The factory listed the 370-bhp/350-cid engine early in the model year, found they couldn't get all the pieces without depriving the Z/28 market, and cancelled. But before they did the factory shop manuals came out. All the engine specifications were listed."

It wasn't the first time a desirable Corvette option was listed early on then erased. And it wouldn't be the last time that fiberglass fans would be teased with a hot new engine only to see it yanked back out of their reach. But unlike the big-block boys, who even then were licking their lips in anticipation of the promised LS-7 454, mouse motor club members in 1970 got a second chance at their carrot on a string. Better late than never.

The LT-1 engine option was priced at $447.60 in 1970. Included in that deal were the big-valve cylinder heads that had been staples around the Corvette's top-performance small-block parts bin dating back to the fuelie's days. Intake valves were 2.02-inchers; exhausts measured 1.60 inches in diameter. These hot heads were also machined for screw-in rocker studs

and used hardened-steel pushrod guideplates. Pushing those rods was an aggressive mechanical cam that dialed in at 317 degrees duration on the intake side, 346 for the exhaust, with 96 degrees of overlap. Valve lift was 0.459 inches intake, 0.485 exhaust.

Four-bolt main bearing caps held a forged crank in place at the block's bottom end. Connecting rods were also forged, as were the aluminum TRW pistons. Compression was a molecule-mashing 11:1. An aluminum high-rise dual-plane intake went on top, itself crowned by a massive model 4150 Holley four-barrel rated at 800 cubic feet per minute. LT-1 Corvettes delivered in California used a slightly different 4150 Holley (the front fuel bowl was vented) to work with the Evaporative Emission Control (EEC) equipment required by that state's clean air cops. At the other end of the process were the big-block's 2.5-inch exhaust pipes in place of the 2-inch tubes normally found behind other 350 small-blocks. Ignition was transistorized by Delco.

Those 370 ponies arrived at 6,000 rpm. Maximum torque of 380 ft-lb came on at 4,000 revs. According to Van Valkenburgh's *Sports Car Graphic* test, this power translated into a 6.7-second ride from rest to 60 miles per hour. *Car Life*'s leadfoots managed 14.17 clicks in the quarter-mile, topping out at 102.2 miles per hour. Of course both the L-88 427 before and the LS-6 454 to come could break into the 13-second bracket with ease. But remember, there was more to the LT-1's appeal than brute

Corvette performance turned a historic corner in 1992 when Chevrolet engineers introduced yet another milestone small-block V-8 for America's only sports car. And to mark this milestone, the division's image-conscious labelmakers reached back in time for a name familiar to anyone who has followed the rich 45-year history of the popular Chevy small-block.

In the 1960s, the supreme small-block was the L-84 327, the fabled "fuelie" V-8, rated at 375 horsepower. During the power-outage years of the late-1970s, the only name that mattered was L-82. In between came the legendary LT-1 350, the small-block that left many big-block owners believing that size indeed doesn't matter.

Recycling famous Corvette options codes was nothing new when the time came to christen Chevrolet's redesigned 5.7-liter V-8 in 1992. The ZR-1 label, first used in small numbers in 1970, was dusted off in 1990 for the "King of the Hill" Corvette with its sensational dual-overhead-cam, 32-valve LT5 V-8. Two years later Chevrolet officials opted to bring back the LT-1 tag for its latest, greatest small-block. Only this time they dropped the hyphen.

It didn't take long for Corvette buyers in 1992 to recognize that the "dehyphenated" LT1 was more than worthy of the name. According to Dave McLellan, the new-generation small-block earned its revered recognition because of its strength—it was easily more powerful than the original LT-1, which, at 370 horses, ranked right up with the mightiest mouse motors

ever built. Consider the name choice a matter of passing the crown along to the latest ruler.

Maximum output for the 1992 LT1 was 300 horsepower at 5,000 rpm; maximum torque was 330 ft-lb at 4,000 rpm. Okay, 300 obviously isn't greater than 370. But remember, advertised outputs before 1972 were gross numbers; along with often being a little on the inaccurate side, they also were dynoed out at the flywheel with no accessory drive drag or external friction losses taken into account. Today's much more honest figures are net ratings; that is, they represent real power delivered right to the road.

As it was, comparing the LT1 with its LT-1 predecessor mattered not at all to drivers who were only familiar with the L98 small-block in their 1991 Corvettes. This time basic arithmetic did apply. Three-hundred horses did dwarf the 245 produced by the L98 350. And if you didn't believe the stats, you could certainly trust the seat of your pants. The LT1 punch literally represented a rebirth for the Corvette in 1992.

The engine itself was surely a rebirth. Next to nothing interchanged between LT1 and L98. Block height, bore spacing, and displacement carried over in the best tradition of the Chevy small-block. Essentially everything else, however, was drawn up on a clean sheet of paper.

Chevrolet's small-block V-8 engineering team was inspired by the ZR-1 Corvette's LT5 V-8. The 5.7-liter LT5 initially produced 375 horses and was later boosted up to 405 horsepower in 1993. While the standard 5.7-liter Corvette small-block was

Chevrolet did away with the hyphen when it dusted off the LT-1 moniker for the Corvette's new standard small-block V-8 in 1992. Helping the wonderfully efficient LT1 350 pump out 300 real horses was the first standard dual exhaust system seen since the Corvette switched to catalytic converters in 1975.

LT1 performance quickly filtered down Chevrolet's performance pecking order after its 1992 introduction. In 1993, a 275-horsepower LT1 became the Z28 Camaro's meat and potatoes. Then in 1994, the new Impala SS (right) debuted with Corvette power beneath its sinister black hood. The Impala SS LT1 was rated at 260 horsepower.

a much more conventional pushrod, two-valve motor, McLellan's engineers recognized that they could squeeze considerably more out of it. Goals for updating the L98 V-8 included at least 50 more horsepower and a higher, flatter, longer torque curve from an engine that at the same time offered increased fuel economy and improved reliability. Tighter external dimensions and quieter running were also among priorities.

India-born Anil Kulkarni was the man given the task of reaching these goals. His engineering team did so and then some. The LT1 became an instant overnight sensation, and not just as the Corvette's heart and soul. In 1993, a 275-horse version of the LT1 helped the redesigned Camaro unseat the 5.0-liter HO Mustang as the performance market's "best bang for the buck." That was followed by a still-hot 260-horsepower LT1 for the Impala SS sport sedan in 1994.

Keys to the LT1's success were improved-flow aluminum heads, 10.2:1 compression, and a much more aggressive roller-lifter cam compared to the L98. Other improvements included a lowered overall height (the better to fit beneath the Corvette's low hoodline) and an unconventional reverse-flow cooling system that delivered coolant from the radiator to the heads first, then the block. This reverse-flow cooling improved combustion efficiency and precision, which in turn benefited both performance and fuel economy.

The LT1 5.7-liter V-8 was joined by an even hotter 330-horsepower LT4 variant in 1996, the last year for Chevrolet's latest legendary small-block. With the arrival of the redesigned C5 Corvette in 1997 came yet another redesigned powerplant, the LS1, leaving the LT1 to retire for a second time. Like its forerunner, its place in automotive Valhalla is guaranteed.

strength. Much more.

Ordering the LT-1 option meant a stiffer suspension was also thrown in as part of the deal, which only further enhanced the small-block Corvette's already nimble nature. "Corvette handling is superior, with any engine," claimed Car Life's test, "and the LT-1 is the best of the bunch. The weight balance is a perfect 50/50 with the small-block engine. The 454 Corvette uses a rear anti-roll bar, to compensate for the weight balance. The 350 Corvette doesn't need it, because there is no problem for which to compensate."

Other comparing critics weren't so kind to the 454 Corvette, which in LS-6 trim in 1971 weighed in at about 300 pounds more than the LT-1. Stiffer springs and an extra sway bar simply couldn't correct the big-block's forward weight bias. "Despite these changes to compensate for the larger engine, the 454 proved to be quite unpredictable and unsettling on the track," concluded Koch in a 1972 Motor Trend base-350/LT-1/big-block run-off. Veteran Corvette racer Tony DeLorenzo, who did all the hotshoe work for that triple-car test, found this out firsthand. "The 454 really got it on in the power department," he told Koch. "However, of the three cars it is the poorest handling. It is a wildly oversteering car, particularly in the fast corners, where it had the tendency to want to get away from you." Physical laws are never broken, at least in most states.

Perhaps the bravest, boldest claim concerning LT-1 handling came from Koch after comparing the 370-horse Corvette to a Porsche 911E for Motor Trend's May 1970 issue. "Off the strip and onto the road course, this is where the Porsche should reign supreme," began Koch. "For years now the words Porsche and handling have been synonymous." Okay, tell us something we didn't know, Chuck. He did. "Here is where we experienced the biggest surprise of the test. The Corvette was just as fast, if not faster through the corners as the Porsche."

Most Americans probably also felt the 1970 LT-1 Corvette was every bit as cool, if not cooler than the Porsche. They were wrong in one respect. Air conditioning could not be installed when the 370-horse 350 was ordered. Nor could the Turbo Hydra-Matic. "Chevrolet is telling you something," explained Car Life's LT-1 review. "You cannot get an automatic transmission, air conditioning or power-assisted

the LT-1's own hot-blooded temperament, something any high-compression engine lives with. Keeping that blood from boiling was tough enough without a compressor pulley to crank. Why push its luck?

As for the automatic exclusion, who cared? A stick was the only choice for any sports car, and in the LT-1's case that choice was limited to two four-speeds: the wide-ratio M20, or the close-ratio M21 box. Standard rear gear ratios behind the transmissions were 3.55:1 for former, 3.70:1 for the latter. The 3.55:1 "economy" ratio was an optional choice for the close-ratio trannie, as were stump-yanking 4.11:1 cogs. Optional rear-axle accompaniment for the wide-ratio four-speed came in 3.36:1 and 3.70:1 ratios.

A third four-speed, the gnarly M22 "Rock Crusher," was also available to LT-1 buyers in 1970, but only by way of the race-ready ZR-1 package. That Chevrolet later applied this now-famous label to its King of the Hill Corvette for the 1990s was no coincidence. The first-edition ZR-1 was no pretender to the throne. In its day, it surely stood as the supreme small-block Corvette, and that may have been selling it a tad short.

Some even consider the LT-1/ZR-1 to be a "small-block L-88" of sorts. No, it didn't have aluminum heads or upwards of 500 horsepower. But it also didn't have that cranky, cantankerous nature and all those extra big-block pounds up front, either. Like the L-88, the ZR-1 was a complete, ready-for-the-track package with a mean and nasty chassis that could both take punishment and dish it out with the best of 'em. Although big-blocks could still out-accelerate

Chevrolet was able to let loose one more LT-1 Corvette in 1972 before the handwriting on the wall let everyone in on the story—the days of truly hot, high-winding V-8s, small- or big-block, would soon be over.

steering. It's hard to find mechanical reason for all of these exclusions. The same engine comes with an automatic in the Z/28, and the bigger Corvettes turn 6,500 rpm and come with the Corvette-only power steering. Our suspicion is that the keen types at Chevrolet just don't want to waste all their engine and chassis work on somebody who drives with his fingerprints."

Maybe so, but leaving off the air conditioning compressor was the only thing to do considering all the cooling problems that had been inherent in the C3 design from the beginning. Compounding that natural fact was

Air conditioning ducts were not things many LT-1 buyers could brag of nearly 40 years ago. No 1970–1971 LT-1 Corvettes were fitted with the cool option. And it wasn't until well into the 1972 run that engineers were finally able to make the combo work. Some estimates put cool-running 1972 LT-1 Corvette production at 240. Others claim 286 were built.

The LT-1 option's price hit $483 in 1972. Still, 1,741 buyers with a need for small-block speed anted up for the last "mouse that roared." This particular 1972 LT-1 played a cameo role in the movie *Apollo 13*, this even though the actual Apollo 13 drama unfolded in 1970.

this macho mouse-motored machine, they had another thing coming in the curves. If the "standard" LT-1 was indeed the "best of all possible Corvettes," then the ZR-1 truly was as good as it gets.

Unlike its modern counterpart, the first ZR-1 attracted very little attention in 1970. Few noticed in part because the option wasn't included in brochures—by most accounts, it wasn't officially mentioned in company paperwork until it appeared in a Chevrolet Motor Vehicle Price Schedule dated April 1, 1970. Even fewer chose the option once they did find it; this was perhaps due to its $965.95 asking price. Apparently the first LT-1/ZR-1 wasn't built until February 1970. Only 24 more rolled out of St. Louis that year.

Footnoted in that price schedule as an "in-dicated change" for the 1970 options list, the "ZR-1 Special Purpose Engine" was "not recommended for normal traffic situations." The equipment list went like this: "Not available when power windows, power steering, air conditioning, audio alarm system, rear window defroster, wheel covers, or radio is ordered. Includes 370-horsepower 350-ci engine, special four-speed close-ratio transmission, HD power brakes, full transistor ignition system, aluminum radiator, special springs with matching shock absorbers, special front and rear stabilizer bars." Since no radio was present, no shielding was needed for the distributor and spark plug wires.

Three items on that list were exclusive to the ZR-1 Corvette, and all three were carry-overs from the L-88s of 1967–69. The F41

With compression lowered to 9:1 and output now listed as a net figure, the LT-1 was rated at 255 horsepower in 1972. Also note the absence of an engine decal—no Corvette V-8s in 1972 had them, probably because Chevy engineers were not at all proud of the new decompressed, net-rated numbers. Barely discernible in this shot is Zora Duntov's autograph on the air cleaner lid. Duntov had actually specified this car to be the test mule for the LT-1/air conditioning combination. It was the first sweat-free LT-1 Corvette built.

special suspension and J56 heavy-duty brakes, like the aforementioned M22 four-speed, were not offered for any other model in 1970.

Standard Sharks were not known for their ride right out of the box, and the beefed-up LT-1 was even less respectful of seat-of-the-pants responses. Imagine, then, how rough and ready the ZR-1 was. Shorter, stiffer coils up front and a seven-leaf rear spring made up the F41 additions. Spring rates were nearly doubled. Although both front and rear heavy-duty sway bars were mentioned, no ZR-1s have ever been spotted wearing a bar in back.

The J56 brakes included the J50 power booster, heavy-duty Delco-Morraine four-piston calipers and fade-resistant metallic linings. Front pads were fixed more firmly in place by two mounting pins each, compared to the rear pads, which typically only used one pin. Cast-iron caliper mount braces were added up front to restrict vibration during hard stops. This brake system was all but identical to the L-88's save for the fact that its dual-circuit master cylinder didn't incorporate a proportioning valve.

The brakes, suspension, and gearbox weren't the ZR-1's only ties to the L-88. The two also shared a heavy-duty nodular-iron flywheel and leg-cramping 10.5-inch clutch. Measuring only 12.75 inches across, compared to the stock LT-1's 14-inch unit, the ZR-1's smaller flywheel helped the high-winding 350 wind up even easier by reducing the rotating mass it had to sling around. Installing this flywheel, in turn, required a smaller bellhousing and the L-88's high-torque starter motor. Another L-88 piece, the ZR-1's large-capacity Harrison aluminum radiator, dated back to the first Mk IV motor Corvette, the 425-horse 396 in 1966. It was fitted with a fan shroud to further aid cooling.

The ZR-1 package itself was fitted to both coupes and convertibles, and it was offered each year the LT-1 was. News in 1971 included a price increase to $1,010 and the introduction of a big-block running mate, the ZR-2. For this year only, the ZR-1 shared its Rocker Crusher four-speed with another Corvette, the LS-6 model. The 12 LS-6/ZR-2 Corvettes built were joined by only 8 LT-1/ZR-1s in 1971.

Corvette brochures finally acknowledged the ZR-1 in 1972, and production for that final year "soared" to 20. These cars all came without fan shrouds with the intention being to once and for all re-emphasize the obvious fact that ZR-1 Corvettes were "not recommended for normal traffic situations." Extra cooling capability via that shroud wasn't needed as long as a ZR-1 stayed in the fast lane, preferably on a racetrack. Transistorized ignition, initially mentioned in 1972 paperwork, was also deleted that year.

Chevrolet's first ZR-1 Corvette retired along with the LT-1 after 1972. Tightening emissions controls, soaring insurance costs, and rising fuel prices all helped ring the death knell for the big, bad small-block. First, its sky-high 11:1 compression was brought back down to earth in 1971, dropping to 9:1. Advertised horses, in turn, fell to 330 (at a slightly lower 5,600 rpm), while the LT-1 option price jumped to $483. When gross horsepower numbers were replaced by net figures in 1972, the LT-1's advertised maximum output shrank even further to 255 horsepower. Maximum torque was 360 ft-lb in 1971, 280 in 1972, both again arriving at 4,000 rpm.

LT-1 buyers were treated to one last surprise just before the car's demise. In July 1971, a build order was issued for an "air conditioning and engine cooling development vehicle" to test whether or not an A/C compressor could peacefully coexist with the solid-lifter small-block. This car was built in September and delivered to the Engineering Center in Warren, Michigan, "to be used for experimental purposes and/or industrial processing." From there it went to GM's Mesa Proving Grounds in Arizona for some serious testing under the sun.

With its wimpy 9:1 compression, the LT-1 was not nearly the same hothead it had been in 1970. Basically all engineers did was add deep-groove pulleys to resist throwing the accessory drive belt at high rpm. The typical LT-1 tach

with its 6,500-rpm redline was also deep-sixed in favor of a rev-counter redlined at 5,600 rpm, this to remind drivers that they needed to keep cool on the throttle to stay cool behind the wheel. Once this War Bonnett Yellow coupe—shown, by the way, on these pages—passed its trial by fire in the desert, Chevrolet officials finally decided to add civilized comfort into the "who-cares-about-the-heat-index?" LT-1 mix.

"So many have asked for it we just had to include the C60 air conditioning as an option," announced *Corvette News* editor Joe Pike in 1972. "If you purchase your Corvette with an LT-1 engine, wide-range transmission and 3.55 ratio rear axle, you now have the option of adding air along with the rest of the goodies. This option, however, is not available with other optional transmissions or axle ratios." The $447.65 C60 option was installed on as many as 240 LT-1 Corvettes during the last four months of 1972 production.

Production of all LT-1s, cool-running or not, was limited, though relatively consistent throughout the three-year run. The numbers read 1,287 in 1970, 1,949 in 1971, and 1,741 in 1972. Although some magazines, in typical fashion, spoke too soon concerning the arrival of a fourth LT-1 Corvette in 1973, anyone with eyes could've recognized that the days of solid lifters and huge Holley four-barrels were over. The mouse that roared would roar no more.

Chevrolet wasn't about to unveil one of the greatest small-block V-8s (if not the greatest) ever built without it being dressed for the occasion. Special valve covers and the expected chrome-topped open-element air cleaner were part of the LT-1 deal. *Chevrolet Motor Division*

Chapter 5

SOFT TOUCHES
The "Bumperless" Years Begin in 1973

Despite press predictions to the contrary, no radical changes were ever made beneath the C3 Corvette's skin. While a new nose was added in 1973, followed by a revised tail in 1974, the basic platform remained all but identical to its 1963 forerunner.

We said it before and we'll say it again—"If it ain't broke, don't fix it." Actually, a GM board member had said it best in June 1972 after viewing one of Duntov's midengine prototypes at the Milford Proving Grounds. "What do you want a new car for?" he blurted out. "You're selling all you can make right now."

Indeed, the 1973 Corvette did a hotcake impersonation like no Corvette ever before on the way to becoming the first of the breed to break the 30,000-unit sales barrier. In a standard 12-month model run, that is. Remember, John DeLorean had "cheated" in 1969. Two months after the former Pontiac chief took over as Chevrolet general manager on February 1, the St. Louis assembly line was shut down by a strike, one of eight UAW work stoppages experienced by GM plants nationwide at the time. The St. Louis strike lasted from April 10 to June 9. Once the Corvette line restarted, DeLorean decided to make up for lost ground. Normally, 1970 production would have begun in September 1969. But Chevy's new general manager put 1970's startup on hold and let the 1969 run continue until December, resulting in that asterisk-marked 38,762-unit sales record.

On the flipside, 1970's late start in January, coupled with yet another plant shutdown from April 6 to May 6—this one brought on by a parts shortage caused by a Teamsters strike—resulted in a drastic drop in production following 1969's sky-high output. The final score for 1970 read only 17,316 Corvettes, the lowest total since 1962. But from then on yearly sales didn't stop increasing until 1978.

As mentioned earlier, the downside to the record-setting production runs in 1968 and 1969 was a startling lack of quality control. DeLorean's predecessor, Pete Estes, temporarily added a third shift at the St. Louis plant in 1968 to speed things along, with the result being a new calendar-year (both 1968 and 1969 models) production record of 32,473 Corvettes—the first 30,000+ January-to-December run in the car's 15-year history. Around-the-clock production also resulted in some of the most shoddily-built Corvettes of all time. A 1970 *Road & Track* survey discovered that "the worst thing about Corvettes, according to the owners, is the workmanship—or the lack of it." *R&T*'s pollsters talked to 177 owners and found that 18 percent of those who drove 1963–67 models felt workmanship was the worst feature. Forty percent of 1968–69 owners picked production quality as the worst feature of their cars.

Although workmanship would improve considerably after 1970, keeping ahead of growing demand would still occasionally compromise production standards—which simply had to remain high for a car the likes of the Corvette. F. James McDonald helped make quality control an even tougher task. A manufacturing

Dwindling demand helped convince Chevrolet to give up on the convertible Corvette after 1975. This Bright Yellow droptop was one of only 4,629 topless models built that year, compared to 33,836 coupes. An open-air Corvette wouldn't return until 1986.

The first major change since 1968 came in 1973 when the Corvette received a new plastic front end. Beneath that monochromatic nose was a structure guaranteed to let the car bounce back from 5-mile-per-hour collisions. The 1973 Corvette's tail remained identical to the 1972's.

Before 1973, the only Corvettes with functional induction systems were the "Airbox" models of the 1950s and the L-88s and ZL-1s of 1967–69. New for 1973 was a functional hood that allowed air pressure that formed at the base of the windshield to force its way through a duct to the carburetor.

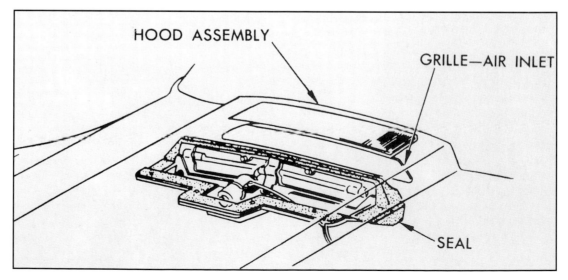

HOOD ASSEMBLY

GRILLE—AIR INLET

SEAL

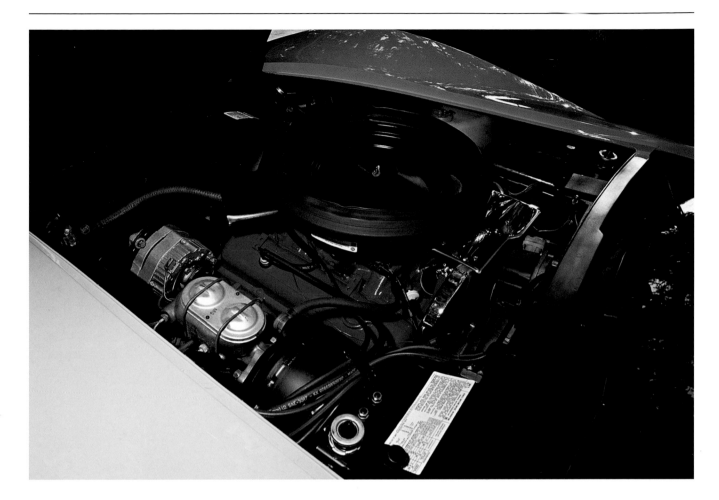

specialist and former head at Pontiac, McDonald took over as Chevrolet general manager on October 1, 1972. In 1974, McDonald gave the go-ahead to pick up St. Louis' production pace from eight Corvettes an hour to nine. Fortunately this move did not lead the Corvette down to the roughshod depths of 1968 and 1969. Just as it had done in 1973, the 1974 Corvette copped honors as the "Best All-Around Car" in Car and Driver's annual readers pole. As it was, McDonald wasn't around to witness the results of his decision either way—former Cadillac exec Robert Lund moved over to Chevrolet to take F. James' place in December 1974.

Actually McDonald had little choice but to step up the production pace in 1974. Growing customer demand warranted the increase. Even with its four-month advantage, the 1969 sales standard probably would have been topped in 1973 had St. Louis been able to build Corvettes fast enough. The 1973 calendar-year run—32,616 cars—was a new record. The final 1973 model-year tally—30,464 Corvettes—represented only

what the assembly line could bear. Another 8,200 orders were returned to dealers unfilled.

Supply continued to soar each year thereafter. Chevrolet sold 37,502 1974 Corvettes, followed by another 38,465 1975 models. The 40,000 plateau went by the boards the following year as a new all-time high was established at 46,558 units. Yet another record came in 1977 as 49,213 Corvettes rolled off the St. Louis line. Interestingly it had taken 15 years for Chevrolet to build its first quarter-million Corvettes. Hitting the half-million mark required only eight more years. The 250,000th example, a Riverside Gold convertible, was built on November 7, 1969. Had things been normal, this milestone machine would have been a 1970 Corvette. But due to DeLorean's extended run, it remained a '69 model. The 500,000th Corvette, a white coupe, was later driven off the line by Robert Lund on March 15, 1977.

"The St. Louis plant is operating two nine-hour shifts daily and working overtime two Saturdays a month just to meet sales demand," said Lund that day. "Current demand is running more

Only three engines were offered for the 1973 Corvette: the base 190-horsepower L-48 350, the 250-horsepower L-82 350, and the 275-horsepower LS-4 454. All three, even the L-48 shown here, were topped by an air cleaner that sealed to the hood's underside, this because standard equipment beginning in 1973 included an air-induction hood.

Difficulties forming the body-colored tail cap left Chevrolet with no choice but to create the thing in two pieces. The luggage rack on this 1974 454 Corvette was a dealer-installed option. The bright exhaust tips are owner-installed preferences.

Things came and went for the 1974 Corvette. This year was the first for a rubber bumper in back and the last for the 454 V-8. Chevrolet cancelled the big-block option after selling 3,494 454 Corvettes, including this coupe, in 1974.

than 29 percent ahead of last year." Predicting yet another Corvette sales record was even easier than shooting fish in a barrel in 1977.

Although it paled in comparison to its 1968–72 forerunners from a power perspective, the second of the C3 Corvette's three "five-year plans" clearly ended with a bang unlike anything heard before. On top of showing production increases for each year from 1973 to 1977, those last two record runs still rank third (1977) and fifth (1976) on the Corvette's all-time sales success scoreboard.

Recognizing those three groups is easy enough. The first, spanning 1968–72, had traditional chrome bumpers at both ends. The 1973–77 Corvettes introduced body-colored, crash-proof bumper systems. Corvettes built from 1978 to 1982 featured a new fastback glass rear roof section. All groups were based on the same platform introduced in 1968, and all still showed off Bill Mitchell's "Coke-bottle" body, at least in the middle.

Trading that classic chrome bumper for a urethane-covered, energy-absorbent front end was the result of new federal automotive safety standards that specified that all 1973 cars be able to bounce back from 5-mile-per-hour impacts. Beneath that monochromatic plastic nosepiece was a steel bumper beam attached to the frame by two ductile steel "Omark" draw bolts. If everything worked right, light collision energy was absorbed by the permanent deformation of the steel beam, coupled with the Omark bolts extrusion through two corresponding dies incorporated into the mounting points on the frame. Both the squished bolts and bent bar required replacement after a 5-mile-per-hour bump, but the plastic nose simply rebounded back into shape, hopefully none the worse for wear. Further safety enhancement was found inside the 1973 Corvette's doors where steel guard beams were added to protect occupants from side impacts.

Even more protection was added in 1974 when the 1973 energy-absorbing nose design was repeated in back. In place of that familiar duck-tail rear and twin chrome bumpers was another resilient plastic cap, this one molded in two pieces. In 1975 the Corvette's body-colored end cap was redone in one piece without that telltale seam down the middle. Beneath that solid cap, a new aluminum bumper bar was attached to the frame with twin hydraulic cylinders. At the same time, the 1975 Corvette was also fitted with a new plastic honeycomb framework beneath its nose to help supply additional low-speed cushioning.

Amazingly all this extra reinforcement, steel or otherwise, didn't add on nearly as many pounds as most detractors feared early on. Reportedly that plastic-covered bumper system up front—which stretched total length by 3 inches—only increased overall weight by 35 pounds in 1973. All told, the typical 1973–77 Corvette curb weight went up about 250 pounds compared to its 1968–72 predecessor.

The 1973 nose job also included a new hood. Like the L-88 hood of 1967–69, this fiberglass lid incorporated ductwork that drew in cooler, denser air from the high-pressure area at the base of the windshield—but only at times when that pressure was truly high. Once a heavy foot depressed the throttle linkage beyond a certain point, a switch activated a solenoid, which in turn opened a flap hidden beneath a grille at the hood's trailing edge.

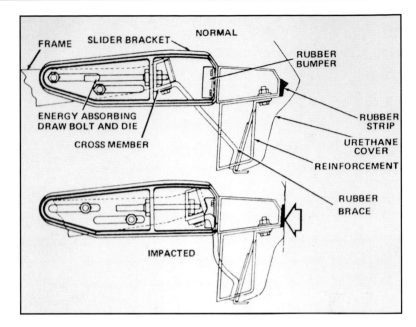

In the beginning, both the front and rear bumper systems worked the same beneath those plastic covers—a long bolt and die destroyed each other to help absorb the punishment. This system was refined a few times along the way.

Stripped of compression and hounded by everyone from insurance agents to safety crusaders to fuel conservationists, the Corvette's Mk IV big-block finally took its last ride in 1974 after leading the way since 1965. Output for the LS-4 454 in 1974 was 270 horsepower. Notice that this 1974 454 Corvette is missing its standard-issue plug wires and ever-present ignition shielding.

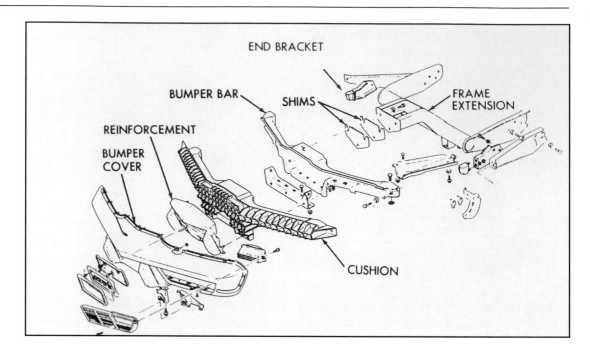

The Corvette's soft nose was refined in 1975 to include a special "honeycomb" cushion to help better resist minor bumps and collisions.

END BRACKET

BUMPER BAR

SHIMS

FRAME EXTENSION

REINFORCEMENT

BUMPER COVER

CUSHION

Opening this flap allowed that denser air to whistle directly to the air cleaner, which was sealed to the hood's underside by a rubber doughnut.

Along with allowing Corvette engines to breathe easier at top end, the new standard hood also did away with a Shark feature that had had many witnesses shaking their heads from its inception in 1968. The 1973 Corvette hood ran all the way back to the windshield un-interrupted, thus doing away with the pop-up panel that had formerly hidden the hideaway wipers on 1968–72 models. Called "GM Futu-rama styling at its worse" by *Car and Driver*, that panel was too slow and clunky and didn't always cooperate as designed. It was also a waste of weight-adding machinery considering that the wipers could simply hide beneath an extended hood's rear lip and operate without additional moving parts, as demonstrated effectively enough in 1973.

Modifications in 1976 did away with the C3 hood's cowl flap, which apparently whistled too loudly for most drivers. In place of the sole-noid-activated induction setup was a simpler system that rammed in airflow through a duct that ran forward over the radiator support to pick up some of the radiator's cooling breezes. Even though the 1976 Corvette's hood no longer used the cowl-induction equipment it still kept the intake grille. That opening wasn't deleted until 1977.

Okay, so the cowl-induction hood did make some unwanted noise. But the rest of the revamped 1973 Corvette was easier on the ears overall compared to its 1968–72 predecessors. Larger mufflers were installed to tone down the exhaust note and extra sound deadener was added both under the hood and in the interior cabin's floor and side panels. The exhausts were tamed even further in 1974 with the addition of two small resonators.

The 1973 Corvette was also easier on the seat of the pants. New rubber cushioned body mounts were added to reduce the amount of vi-brations transferred from the road to the driver through the frame. Also helping reduce ride harshness were the standard steel-belted radial tires introduced for 1973. Both Firestone and Goodyear supplied these GR70-15 treads, which ran more smoothly at highway speeds and improved wet-weather braking perform-ance. On the other hand, magazine road tests showed that the radials reduced maximum cor-nering ability, as well as maximum stopping power on dry surfaces.

Initial plans in 1973 included offering op-tional aluminum wheels, RPO YJ8, to comple-ment those radials and to help offset some of that extra federally mandated fat. Each YJ8 rim would have cut off 8 pounds of unsprung weight—had they been installed. Manufactur-ing gremlins, however, forced a recall of these wheels after about a couple of hundred sets were

cast because quality wasn't up to snuff. Sound familiar? A similar situation occurred in 1963 when Chevrolet first tried to introduce cast-aluminum knock-off wheels for the Sting Ray. Just as some of those knock-offs surely made it into the wild 10 years before, Chevy paperwork in 1973 showed that as many as four Corvettes apparently were delivered with YJ8 wheels. Additional sets may have "slipped out the back-door" as well.

RPO YJ8 didn't become an official (read: successfully produced) option until 1976. The package included four aluminum wheels with a standard steel spare to keep the cost down. The price in 1976 was $299. It was $321 in 1977. Production was 6,253 for the former, 12,646 for the latter.

Third-generation Corvette owners who understood the value of reducing unsprung weight and cared little about harsh rides were treated to yet another new option, RPO Z07. Offered from 1973 to 1975, the Z07 package included considerably stiffer springs and shocks at both ends, a thicker front sway bar (a rear sway bar was also listed), and heavy-duty power brakes with dual-pin-mounted pads up front and fade-resistant

In 1975 the Corvette received a one-piece rear body section.

Another era in Corvette history came to an end in 1975. Sixty-five-year-old Zora Arkus-Duntov officially retired on January 1, after 21 years and 7 months with General Motors. Two decades before he had boldly written Chevrolet chief engineer Ed Cole about a job after seeing the Corvette prototype on stage at GM's Motorama auto show in New York. "Now there's potential," he remembered thinking in a 1967 *Hot Rod* interview. "I thought it wasn't a good car yet, but if you're going to do something, this looks good." Duntov's letter led to a job as an assistant staff engineer at Chevrolet beginning May 1, 1953. "Not for [the] Corvette or anything of that sort," he told *Hot Rod*'s Jim McFarland, "but for research and development and future stuff."

"Considering his present stature, it is surprising to find that Duntov was not a part of the original Corvette project," began a December 1972 *Car and Driver* account of Zora's latest achievements. "However, he was soon drawn into it and he is certainly the architect of its performance image that began to emerge with the 1956 models. Since then his influence has grown to the point where he is known worldwide as the Father of the Corvette, a position all the more remarkable in Detroit, the land of the committee car. So it follows, then, that if you are to understand the Corvette you must not only drive it with an open mind but also hear of it from Duntov."

Zora Arkus-Duntov joined General Motors in 1953 and retired in 1975.

"That was the first Corvette that reflected my thinking," he told *Road & Track*'s Allan Girdler in 1989, in reference to the revamped, restyled 1956 model. After "fiddling on the side" (his words) in 1953 and 1954, Duntov was officially named Chevrolet's director of high-performance vehicle design and development in 1956, with his main focus of course being the division's highest-performance vehicle. His legendary, long-running "Duntov cam" appeared the following year, as did another major milestone—Ramjet fuel injection. Zora worked alongside engineer John Dolza to create the fabled "fuelie" small-block, which then led the way as the Corvette's top performance option up through 1964.

After only a few years on the job, Duntov was widely recognized as the man with his thumb firmly planted on the Corvette's pulse. Yet he wasn't officially named Corvette chief engineer until 1968, this after some bureaucratic bumbling had temporarily cut him out of the loop late in the C3 development process. From 1968 to 1974, he reigned supreme.

For those who've always wondered, but were afraid to ask, the Father of the Corvette got his name as a result of himself having two dads. The son of Russian parents, Zora Arkus was born in Belgium on Christmas day, 1909. Later, after returning to her hometown, by then known as Leningrad, Zora's mother divorced and remarried Josef Duntov. Both Zora and his brother, Yura, then took on the hyphenated last name out of respect to Misters Arkus and Duntov.

Those two monikers were merged even tighter together after the brothers fled Europe just ahead of Hitler's blitz in December 1940. In 1942 Zora teamed up with Yura to open a machine shop in New York. This endeavor quickly grew into the Ardun Mechanical Corporation—Ardun, of course, being short for Arkus-Duntov.

The company's main claim to fame was the legendary overhead-valve Ardun head conversion for Ford's flathead V-8. The plan was to produce these exceptional cylinder heads for Ford, but the deal fell through. No worry. British sports car builder Sydney Allard began offering the Ardun-head Ford V-8 in his J2 sports racers in 1949. Zora himself went to work for Allard in England soon afterward. He also drove an Allard racer at Le Mans in 1952.

Zora then returned to the States in time to get his first look at a Corvette in January 1953. An avid speed freak dating back to his youngest days, Duntov continued racing even after going to work for Chevrolet. He drove again at Le Mans in 1953, despite Ed Cole's insistence that he stay home and attend to his new position. His job was still there, of course, after the 24-hour race. It also remained intact following the class victories he scored while piloting a Porsche Spyder at Le Mans in

1954 and 1955. From then on, however, driving fast Corvettes remained his prime passion.

A bold race driver. A dashing, unforgettably handsome man who knew how to show off with style. An engineering genius with few equals. A fair-minded gentleman leader. If there was anything bad to say about the man, no one was talking following his death in April 1996.

"I was impressed with his continental poise, sophistication and his honesty and dedication to performance and to his work as an engineer," began Gib Hufstader's respectful homage. "He appreciated people who were very dedicated to doing a good job, to getting the job done. For some of us, it was a dream come true to work with him."

How did a mere mortal pick up where Zora left off in 1975?

The man handed the task of keeping the dream alive was David Ramsay McLellan. McLellan had begun his engineering career in 1959 after graduating from Wayne State University. His first job was in the noise-and-vibration laboratory at GM's Milford Proving Grounds where he demonstrated a knack for developmental design work. Dave moved on to Chevrolet early in 1969 to apply his talents to the new second-generation Camaro. A brief assignment in 1971 had him at GM's Technical Center working on John DeLorean's proposed "K-car" program. To Duntov's distinct dismay, the K-car was intended as a platform combining the Nova, Camaro, and Corvette. After this ill-fated proposal was rightly shot down, McLellan remained at the Tech Center as a full-time chassis engineer for the Camaro/Nova group.

Dave McLellan spent most of 1973 and 1974 at the Massachusetts Institute of Technology's Sloan School of Management. Not only did his GM bosses encourage this move, they also paid for it. Clearly he was being groomed for something big. With his MIT master's degree in hand, he returned to Chevrolet in the summer of 1974 as one of Duntov's staff engineers. Six months later, Zora stepped down and McLellan rose to the post that he already knew was his for the taking.

What wasn't so apparent was how Dave McLellan was going to make his mark on America's only sports car. The 1975 Corvette was, of course, well into its sales run by the time he took the reins. The following year's final product then too was already cast in stone, meaning the 1976 Corvette would follow closely in the tracks of every Shark born since 1968. The same went for the 1977 model. The new regime didn't make a noticeable impact until the Corvette was fitted with "fastback" rear glass in 1978. This minor makeover, however, represented nothing more than make-work, something to pass the time until McLellan's creative juices could boil over into the marketplace. That wouldn't happen for another five years.

The names *Duntov* and *Corvette* had become all but synonymous within three or four years after Zora's arrival at Chevrolet. It took about eight years for the moniker McLellan to edge its way near the household category. Dave first made his presence known in a really big way on March 24, 1983, when he introduced the long-awaited 1984 Corvette

to Californians. The rest of America got its first look at his redesigned C4 on April 21.

C4 development dated back to 1978—a time when Duntov's midengine proposals remained fresh in everyone's minds. Including Zora's first and foremost. Though retired, he still dropped by McLellan's offices in Warren, Michigan, about once a month. The Father not only couldn't just walk away from his baby, he also couldn't quite forget the one dream that was never fulfilled, this even though GM execs had already all but dashed it to pieces.

Michael Lamm explained the situation in his 1983 book, *The Newest Corvette.* "In a 1978 conversation, Zora acknowledged to McLellan that Chevrolet wasn't committed to the midengine concept," he wrote, "although when I questioned Duntov in late 1982, he expressed some disappointment that the new [1984] car had abandoned the midship layout."

McLellan did dabble with a mid-engine mule early on, whether out of respect for the old man or as a product of at least a partial belief that Zora was right. "Partial" because Dave was undoubtedly much more of a realist than Duntov. He knew his bosses would never fund any really radical innovation. "The Stingray kept selling very robustly even into the early 1980s," said McLellan to Lamm in 1983. "And this trend made it harder to sell management on any new Corvette program, front- or rear-engined. Given our limited manufacturing capacity at St. Louis, given that you couldn't market any more cars of the more expensive mid-engine configurations—at the time management wasn't interested in these other sides of the game."

Dave McLellan stepped down in 1992. David Hill then became the Corvette's third chief engineer.

Dave McLellan started his career at GM's Milford Proving Grounds in 1959 and became one of Duntov's staff engineers in the summer of 1974. When Duntov retired in 1975, he assumed control of the Corvette program.

metallic linings all around. Like similar competition-oriented options before it, RPO Z07 was clearly intended for the track, not the street. Thus it could not be ordered with the mundane base 350 small-block or air conditioning. The M21 close-ratio four-speed was also mandatory.

RPO Z07's price was $369 in 1973, $400 in 1974 and 1975. Production figures reflected the option's not-ready-for-prime-time nature. Only 45 Z07 Corvettes were built in 1973, 47 in 1974 and 144 in 1975.

RPO FE7, the Gymkhana suspension package, was far more plentiful, because it was both easier on the wallet and the pants where that wallet resided. Introduced in 1974, it simply included a thickened front sway bar and higher-rate springs—no stiffened shocks or brawny brakes were included. Nor were there any ordering restrictions or additional mandatory options. Standard 350, automatic transmission, air conditioning—it didn't matter, the FE7 option could be added with no questions

asked. Its price? A measly $7 in 1974 and 1975. That figure went up to $35 in 1976, then to $38 in 1977.

In this case, production figures reflected the FE7 package's softer sell, at least from a pricing perspective. While the less-gnarly FE7 group wasn't labeled an off-road option and Z07 was, the former still was not recommended for "casual use." An FE7-equipped Corvette could rattle a tooth or two, yet that apparently didn't hinder buyers who didn't mind trading comfortable kidneys for improved road-hugging capabilities. Chevrolet sold 1,905 FE7 packages in 1974, 3,194 in 1975, 5,368 in 1976, and 7,269 in 1977.

In other 1973–77 news, the removable rear window formerly included on all 1968–72 Corvettes was dropped in favor of fixed glass. Duntov did this to eliminate an unwanted backdraft that would occur at high speeds with windows up and roof panels removed. The breaker-less High Energy Ignition—with its

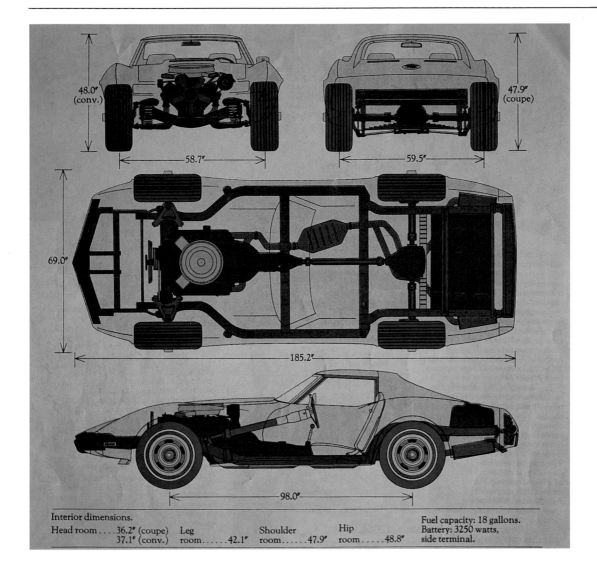

48.0" (conv.)

47.9" (coupe)

58.7"

59.5"

69.0"

185.2"

98.0"

Interior dimensions.
Head room....36.2" (coupe)   Leg   Shoulder   Hip   Fuel capacity: 18 gallons.
            37.1" (conv.)   room......42.1"   room......47.9"   room.....48.8"   Battery: 3250 watts,
                                                                                     side terminal.

Also new for 1975 was a catalytic converter exhaust system. And since only one "cat" was used beneath the car's floorboard, a system of two Y-pipes routed exhaust into a single flow then back into dual mufflers. True dual exhausts wouldn't be seen again beneath a Corvette until the ZR-1 debuted for 1990. Standard duals reappeared for all models behind the LT1 350 in 1992.

hotter, more reliable spark—was made standard in 1975. A steel underpan was added in 1976 to increase rigidity and improve heat insulation. And a lighter (13 pounds or so) Delco Freedom battery joined the standard equipment list that year as well. Finally, the familiar Stingray script was deleted once and for all from Corvette fenders in 1977.

Clearly Corvettes built after 1973 were better cars as far as noise, vibration, and harshness were concerned. That was the idea. Duntov chose to improve his pride and joy as best he could within the rules imposed upon him. In one hand were safety czars' mandates that forced him to add weight to the car. In the other were stringent smog standards that limited how much horsepower he could use to try compensating for those extra pounds. Performance initially was the loser in the deal.

That the sporting crowd continued flocking into the fiberglass fraternity in ever-greater numbers from 1973 to 1977 wasn't exactly indicative of an ever-growing ability to stir the soul during those years. On the contrary, standard V-8 muscle sank to an all-time low: 190 horsepower in 1973, 165 in 1975. Mind you, these were net ratings, but they still represented an unprecedented downturn compared to 1972's 200 SAE net standard horses.

Along with horsepower, the engines themselves began disappearing after 1972. The LT-1's failure to return for 1973 in turn meant the end of the road for solid lifters, those noisy, rev-sensitive mechanical tappets that for more than 15 years had reminded Corvette drivers that the engine beneath that fiberglass hood did indeed mean business. "At first it seems unthinkable," began *Car and Driver*'s December 1972 obit.

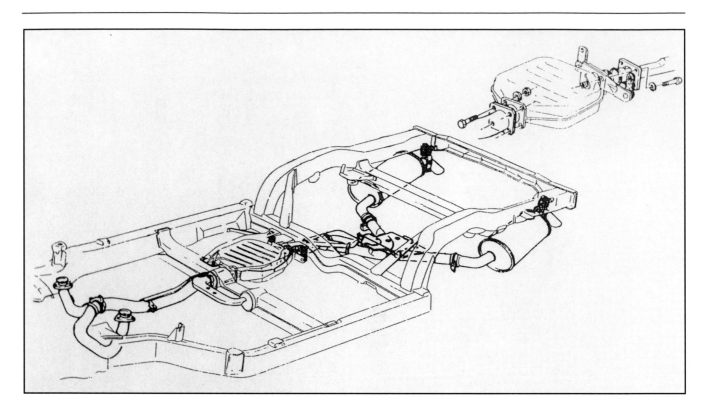

"High winding engines and valve train clatter have been Corvette trademarks since 1956. To the enthusiast, it was those solid lifters that separated the Corvette engines from their weaker passenger car siblings. And now, with the passing of the LT-1, it is reasonable to say that The Corvette Engine no longer exists."

Even after the LT-1's demise, Corvette buyers in 1973 still had three V-8s to chose from, same as in 1972. Joining the base 350 small-block and the optional LS-4 454 big-block was a new RPO code—L-82. Though it filled in the space left behind by the LT-1, the L-82 small-block was actually a descendant of the hydraulic-lifter L-46 350, discontinued after 1970. Featuring 9:1 compression, big-valve heads and a relatively aggressive hydraulic cam, the L-82 350 produced 250 horses, which still stood tall despite *Car and Driver*'s claim that Corvette-style power had blacked out. L-82 compression never slipped during the 1973–77 run, and in fact topped all Corvette engines built in those years. L-82 output in 1974 was again 250 horsepower. But it dropped to 205 in 1975, then leveled out at 210 net horses in 1976 and 1977.

The explanation for the L-82's power outage? Those industrywide (Chevrolet wasn't alone) compression cuts made in 1971 had represented Detroit's first step toward the mandated use of lower-octane unleaded gasoline, which reportedly ran cleaner than the tetraethyl lead-laced jet fuels previously used to keep high-compression Corvette engines alive and well. While the cleaner-running aspects of unleaded gas could've been debated then, and were, the real reason behind the introduction of low-lead fuels in 1971 was to prepare the market for the next wave of federally ordered clean air requirements, scheduled to be met by 1975. To comply with these more stringent emission-control standards, Detroit engineers concocted the contaminant-burning catalytic converter, which didn't mix at all with leaded gasoline.

So it was that the limited availability of low-lead gas in 1971 set the stage for ethyl's swan song. By July 1, 1974, every retail outlet in America "at which 200,000 or more gallons of gasoline was sold during any calendar year beginning with 1971" was required by law to offer unleaded fuel of at least 91 octane.

This requirement, in turn, allowed Chevrolet engineers to introduce a catalytic converter exhaust system for the 1975 Corvette. A single large-capacity converter was installed after a design featuring two smaller units failed durability tests. Two Y-pipes were used to at least preserve the appearance of a sporty dual exhaust system. The first one funneled exhaust flow

Corvettes for 1976 received a steel floorboard section to increase rigidity and improve insulation. The cowl flap induction setup was also traded for a forward-inlet system to reduce noise. Though the hood no longer drew fresh air in from the base of the windshield, the ornamental vent remained for one more year.

from both sides of the engine together into one tube to enter the converter. From there a reversed Y-pipe did the opposite in back to deliver the cleansed spent gases to typical twin mufflers at the tail. Corvette buyers after 1974 could then pretend their cars still had dual exhausts. True duals wouldn't make a comeback until the LT5-powered ZR-1 debuted for 1990. Standard Corvettes were finally refitted with a real dual exhaust system as part of the second-generation LT1 upgrade made for 1992.

The restrictive single-exhaust setup put a severe crimp on things in 1975. Thus the base 350's abysmal 165-horsepower rating and the L-82's corresponding output drop. Fortunately some extra tinkering brought both these ratings back up—180 horsepower for the former, the aforementioned 210 for the latter—for 1976 and 1977. However, no amount of hocus-pocus could've restored the once-mighty Corvette engine that failed to make the 1975 lineup. The Mk IV big-block V-8, the Corvette's toughest engine option since its introduction in 1965, was dropped from the RPO list after 1974.

Even with its low 8.25:1 compression, the LS-5 454's successor, the LS-4, still remained atop of the Corvette's performance pecking order in 1973 with its 275 horsepower. And it stayed there with its 270 horses the following year. Big numbers, however, weren't enough to keep the 454 big-block alive. Diminishing demand for the expensive-to-own, relatively inefficient LS-4 was the common excuse given for its demise.

Zora Arkus-Duntov always understood the logic behind the midengine layout. The design offers various advantages, not the least of which involves getting all that weight off the nose. Reducing the pounds pounding the front wheels lightens up steering effort. This, in turn, means faster manual steering ratios can be used without overtaxing the driver's arms. And moving the engine to the middle not only better balances the

dreams. "The original 6-cylinder car had hardly gotten out of the mold, and Duntov had barely settled in his then-new job in Research and Development, but already different configurations were being considered."

"I came up with a report shortly after," added Zora. "I convinced myself that a car of 40/60 weight distribution doesn't need much to make it well behaved. I remember the

Built in 1959, the CERV I racer/engineering testbed helped lay the groundwork for development of the 1963 Sting Ray's independent rear suspension. It also helped put midengine thinking on the fast track around Chevrolet Engineering. *Chevrolet Motor Division*

load, it can also translate into a preferred lower center of gravity, this because all that motive mass can be mounted closer to the road with no steering or suspension components barring the way. The cockpit can be lowered, too, primarily because the pilot doesn't have to look over a big V-8 perched directly in his line of sight.

Additional advantages were even more obvious to Duntov. "The mass distribution of, say, about 40 [percent] front/60 rear will offer much better traction and handling," he told *Car Life's* Gene Booth in 1968. "You can utilize your power much more accurately."

Or so he thought when GM hired him in May 1953. "Duntov recalls that he was proposing a rear- or midship-mounted engine Corvette to Chevrolet management back in 1954," wrote Booth in his June 1968 account of Zora's hopes and

wording. I said, 'If you inflate the tires corresponding to their respective load, the car is in the ballpark.' Then you have to do a few things; but the car will turn, it will not spin out, and if you make it break away, it will do it slowly and correctably."

So why didn't Chevrolet begin building a superbly handling midengine Corvette then? "My boss felt that it wasn't as simple as that," answered Duntov. Zora's relocated-engine ideal wasn't considered again until 1959. But no one on the street really paid all that much attention when the mid-engine CERV I racer appeared in 1960. After all, this obviously was an engineering experiment. Much the same could be said when the all-wheel-drive CERV II followed in 1964.

Then Duntov proposed yet another mid-engine racer, the GS 3, in April 1964. Also included in that proposal were two lightweight production Corvettes; one with its engine mounted up front, the other with a powerplant located amidships. These ideas never made it off the drawing board, but they did lay the groundwork for more innovative thinking to come.

Duntov's dreams remained just that in 1964. But R&D engineer Frank Winchell's came true, albeit briefly. Created later that year, Winchell's XP-819 Corvette attempted to prove that moving the engine to the tail, Corvair-style, was the way of the future. Track tests proved otherwise.

Winchell then returned to the drawing board in 1967, resulting in the sleek XP-880. This midengine experimental was running by February 1968, then was officially named "Astro II" in preparation for a public introduction at the New York Auto Show in April. Although it looked stunning, the Astro II's wimpy two-speed automatic transaxle—borrowed from a 1963 Pontiac Tempest—ruled out any chances for additional development.

Picking up where Winchell's XP-880 left off was the XP-882, which Duntov began putting together early in 1968. Unlike previous prototypes, the XP-882 featured a transverse-mounted engine. This unique design was nearing testing stages early in 1969 when new Chevrolet general manager John DeLorean cancelled the project. He directed designers instead to try a less expensive course using a more conventional platform based on the Camaro chassis then being readied for 1970.

Fortunately this "Cormaro" idea was itself quickly cancelled after it was learned that both Ford and American Motors would be showing up at the 52nd annual New York Auto Show in April 1970 with their own midengine proposals, the Pantera and AMX/3, respectively. In response, Chevrolet revived the

XP-882 project and put together its own 1970 exhibit labeled simply "Corvette prototype."

"We'll stake our reputation on this being the Corvette of the future," announced a July 1970 *Road & Track* report, "but don't expect it until 1972 at the earliest." Six months later, *R&T's* Ron Wakefield explored the midengine proposal further.

The Reynolds Metals people helped the XP-895 midengine experimental lose some weight with a body made entirely of aluminum. This idea would have never meshed with production realities. *Reynolds Metals Company*

The Italian-styled "2-Rotor" Corvette kicked off the shortlived Wankel development era. Two rotors weren't enough, so Duntov and Gib Hufstader just had to add two more.

Safety nazis be damned, the design team added gullwing doors to the sensational "4-Rotor" Corvette. Duntov and company did manage to extract ample power from the four-rotor setup, but GM gave up on the rotary experiment and opted instead to leave well enough alone. Corvettes to this day remain powered by V-8 engines mounted over the front wheels.

"We have now established beyond a doubt that the car was indeed a prototype for future production—1973, to be exact—and can report full details on the 1973 Corvette," he wrote in the January 1971 issue.

Further toying with the XP-882 platform in 1971 resulted in the more pleasing XP-895. But as much as this prototype looked like the next step into the future, the XP-895 still weighed every bit as much as a regular-production Corvette. To breach this hurdle, DeLorean turned to the Reynolds Metals Company in 1972. Reynolds redid the XP-895 body in aluminum and delivered it to Chevrolet Engineering. A year or so later, Chevy engineers used that lightweight shell to create an XP-895 variant that weighed about 500 pounds less than the original. Costly production processes, however, killed the Reynolds Corvette idea before it ever got rolling.

As for the basic midengine Corvette idea, it was KO'ed more than once. By DeLorean in 1969. By GM's executive board in 1972. But the XP-882 platform just wouldn't die.

Yet another resurrection followed after GM bought out the patent rights to the Wankel rotary engine in November 1970. In June 1971, GM president Ed Cole gave the go-ahead to the XP-897GT project. Wearing a Pininfarina body atop that same transverse-engine chassis, this car, the so-called "2-Rotor Corvette," debuted in September 1973. Duntov never did like the rotary Corvette idea, but he had no choice in the matter.

"Ed Cole was enamored with the Wankel engine," said Zora in a 1980 AutoWeek interview. "And he kept twisting my arm. 'What about a rotary Corvette?' Originally, the rotary engine was intended for the Vega. But the idea of sharing the Vega powerplant with the Corvette was nonsense. Still Cole asked me to produce a rotary Corvette and I was in a dilemma. Then DeLorean comes to styling and looks at the midengine Corvette. He knows already that the decision has been made to produce this Corvette, but with the Wankel engine. I told him it was not powerful enough and he lost his composure. 'You're some genius!' he shouted. 'Invent something!'

Duntov turned to Gib Hufstader, who then did the 2-Rotor job two better. Hufstader's much more powerful "4-Rotor" Corvette debuted one month after the XP-897GT. Using two Wankel engines coupled together, this truly fast gull-winged beauty was, according to Car and Driver, "the betting-man's choice to replace the Stingray." Whether or not that was a good bet was rendered a moot point after Cole announced in September 1974 that GM was postponing the use of the Wankel rotary engine after running into problems getting it emissions certified.

Two years later, the 4-Rotor Corvette's Wankel was replaced by a conventional small-block V-8 as the name was changed to "Aerovette." The body remained the same, as did those tired, old rumors. According to a February 1977 Road & Track prediction, the Aerovette would become the 1980 Corvette. Too bad Chevrolet was still selling conventional Corvettes like there was no tomorrow.

By 1978, Dave McLellan was busy working full-time on the new fourth-generation Corvette—it with its engine mounted up front. Zora had retired three years earlier and his hopes for a world-class midengine Corvette had all but retired with him. As work on the Shark's replacement finally began, Chevrolet officials once and for all decided to put the dream to rest.

Indeed, the painful realities of 50-cent gallons of low-lead and insurance premiums as heavy as car payments did dissuade jet-setters from choosing the LS-4 option in 1973 and 1974. Throw in the fact that the L-82 was both cheaper to insure, better on fuel, and only 25 horses short, and the big picture became obvious. Even though it cost more, the $299 L-82 350 outnumbered the $250 LS-4 454 5,710 to 4,412 in 1973, and 6,690 to 3,494 in 1974. In 1969 Chevrolet had rolled out nearly 16,000 big-block Corvettes. Five years later, bigger apparently was no longer better.

With the 454 in the archives, the Corvette engine lineup was left with only the standard 350 and the optional L-82 in 1975—the first time in 20 years that only two power sources were available. And with the L-82 being the only choice left for buyers wanting the most Chevy engineers had to offer, Chevy's bean-counters couldn't resist upping the RPO ante to $336. The L-82's price jumped (make that soared) again to $481 in 1976, then to $495 in 1977. But apparently the sticker shock wore off quickly. After L-82 sales dropped to 2,372 in 1975, they rebounded to 5,720 in 1976 and 6,148 in 1977.

For some Americans, there was only one drivetrain choice available during those last two years. The L-82 was not offered on 1976 and 1977 Corvettes sold in California because the optional performance V-8 did not meet that state's tougher emissions standards. Four-speed transmissions were also "banned" out West for those years, meaning the only combo a Californian could buy was the 180-horsepower 350 backed by the Turbo Hydra-Matic automatic.

And that auto box wasn't the TH 400 previously used behind all engines. Corvettes fitted with the standard 350 in 1976 and 1977 received the mundane TH 350 as product planners opted not to "waste" the more expensive, heavy-duty Turbo Hydra-Matic on engines that didn't put out enough punishment to merit its use. The TH 400 remained the weapon of choice whenever an L-82 buyer forked over the extra cash for the M40 automatic transmission option in 1976 and 1977. "Heavy" M40 prices were $134 for former, $146 for the latter. The lighter TH 350 M40 package was a no-cost option behind the base 350.

Engines and transmissions weren't the only things to fade from a Corvette buyer's

sight in the 1970s. One year after the last big-block Corvette rolled into the sunset, the same thing happened to the convertible model. GM's explanation this time involved both safety concerns and, again, nose-diving demand. From 1953 to 1962, all Corvettes had been convertibles, and not even the stunning Sting Ray coupe could change the way Americans looked at Chevrolet's two-seater. After nearly matching droptop production its first time out in 1963, the Corvette coupe then lost favor as the wind-in-the-hair crowd temporarily regrouped. The coupe's cut of yearly production was 37.3 percent in 1964, 34.7 in 1965,

Decision-makers drew sharp criticism in 1976 after adding this sport steering to the Corvette's interior. Save for the cross-flag medallion, it was the same four-spoke wheel used in Chevy Vegas.

35.9 in 1966, and 37.1 in 1967. The coupe percentage remained in that same ballpark in 1968 when the Shark body debuted with its removable roof panels.

Stingray sport coupe sales then more than doubled in 1969 as the percentage hit 57.2 percent. It then became the convertible's turn to hold the short end of the stick. Droptop sales went from 18,630 in 1968, to 6,648 in 1970, and to 4,943 in 1973. The convertible's piece of the pie sank from 38.4 percent in 1970, to 32.7 in 1971, 24.1 in 1972, and 16.2 in 1973. Those last 4,629 ragtops built in 1975 represented a mere 12 percent of the total production run that year. Another end of an era? So we all thought. Then. Fortunately topless Corvettes returned to center stage in 1986.

Declining Corvette convertible demand was the result of various factors, not the least of which was a general trend of disinterest felt across the board in Detroit. By 1976, all factory-built American convertibles were history, apparently because comfort-conscious American drivers were growing more spoiled by the day. During the 1960s, staying cool had taken precedence over being cool. High-profilin' open-air touring lost favor while sales of expensive air conditioning options began heating up considerably at decade's end at any dealership near you, be it allied to GM, Ford, or Chrysler.

America's only sports car was no exception. RPO C60, optional air conditioning, was introduced to Corvette customers along with the all-new Sting Ray in 1963. Its price was $421.80. Only 278 buyers (equal to 1.3 percent of the total

1963 Corvette market) were willing to spend that much then. Again, the key word was "then." By 1968 C60 installations were making up 19.8 percent of the production run. In 1969 the figure was 30.6. It was 52.7 in 1971, 70.8 in 1973, and 82.8 in 1975. Once more, as demand picked up, so too did the price. Six years after it first appeared, the Corvette's air conditioning option had only risen $6.90 in cost. The C60 tag then went up to $447.65 in 1970, $452.00 in 1973, $490 in 1975, and $553 in 1977.

Air conditioning's soaring popularity in the 1970s represented just one facet in what many purists felt was the "sissification" of the once-macho fiberglass two-seater. Whatever the case, buyers still kept snapping up more and more Corvettes loaded down with more and more comfort and convenience options. Who could blame them? Horsepower was becoming harder to come by, why not leave that ongoing debate concerning the Corvette's sports car status completely behind and build yourself a sexy luxury GT?

Various other "kinder, gentler" options accordingly experienced their own newfound sales success in the 1970s. Power steering, power brakes and leather appointments, all introduced along with air conditioning in 1963, also jumped up the Corvette pop charts with a bullet. Power windows, added to the options list in 1956, did, too. The percentage of 1963 Sting Rays equipped with RPOs J50 (power brakes) and N40 (power steering) was 15.5 and 14.2, respectively. By 1970 those figures had soared to 53.6 and 68.8, and they didn't stop there. Ninety-seven-point-seven percent of the Corvettes built in 1975 were fitted with optional power steering; 93.1 percent had power brakes.

Power windows were rarely seen during the 1950s. And in 1967 RPO A31 still only found its way into 17.6 percent of the Sting Rays built that year. By 1973 the percentage of A31 power window installations was at 46. It reached 63.8 the following year, 83.1 in 1976, and 90.1 in 1977.

The situation in 1976 became as obvious as it had been in 1970, the year when Chevrolet product planners made Positraction and a four-speed standard equipment. Late in 1976, power steering, power brakes, and the custom interior trim group (with its leather seats) became part of the base Corvette package. All Corvettes built for 1976 featured power brakes, while only 173 hit the streets without power steering. Power steering and brakes were fitted to every 1977 Corvette as standard equipment, and the same would've been said about the custom interior group's leather seats had not Chevrolet also offered leather-trimmed cloth seats at no extra cost that year.

Of course all these additions to the standard package meant a corresponding rise in the base price. While horsepower was on the wane in the 1970s, pricing was riding an increasing curve upward. A Corvette's base sticker edged beyond $6,000 (by $1.50) for the first time in 1974. It jumped to $6,810.10 in 1975, then hit $7,604.85 the following year. In 1977 it was a whopping $8,647.65, this due to the inclusion of that extra dose of standard comfort, convenience, and class. Yet even with such intimidating price hikes customers continued buying their favorite fiberglass dream machine.

Clearly the Corvette thrived in a seller's market from 1973 to 1977. Chevrolet sold so many Corvettes primarily because performance fans had next to nothing else to choose from coming out of Detroit. Basically the only thing on four wheels remotely comparable to the Corvette in those days was Pontiac's Trans Am and, to a lesser degree, Chevy's own Z28 Camaro.

Car and Driver's April 1976 issue even went so far as to compare the Corvette and Trans Am with Ford's little Mustang II Cobra II, Dodge's Dart Sport, and, gulp, Chevy's C-10 Silverado pickup truck in an article titled "Finding the Fastest American Car." At 15.3 seconds, the L-82 Corvette's ET won out, followed closely by the 455 Trans Am's 15.6 time slip. The Trans Am went fastest 0–60, nosing out the Corvette by a tenth with a 7-flat clip. The Corvette took actual Fastest American Car honors at 124.5 miles per hour, followed curiously by the 360-powered Dodge Dart with its 121.6-mile-per-hour top end.

A Corvette fan could've looked at it two ways a quarter century ago. Even with all those power cutbacks, America's only sports car remained America's fastest, best-handling automobile in the 1970s, a time when true speed was truly hard to come by. Yet in a few short years the Corvette was transformed from an intimidating animal into an image-conscious status machine targeted more toward the wannabe crowd than real rally runners.

Perhaps those plastic bumpers said it all. By the late-1970s, Corvettes could have been considered soft touches in more ways than one.

Chapter 6

LIFE IN THE FASTBACK LANE
A New Profile Debuts in 1978

Witnesses who felt things had gotten a touch soft in the Corvette camp in the mid-1970s had another coming at the turn of the next decade. Although engineers in the late 1970s and early 1980s did manage to keep their fingers in the horsepower dyke—no small achievement considering those stifling emissions standards—they had no choice but to give Corvette customers what they wanted. And what they wanted wasn't exactly what Zora Duntov originally had in mind when he began envisioning a future for the fantastic plastic showcar he first stumbled across in December 1953. Then again, Zora was no longer the boss by the time his baby was celebrating its 25th birthday.

"Keeping [customers] content is Dave McLellan's job as the Corvette's chief engineer," explained a December 1978 Car and Driver report on the latest status of America's only sports car. "While he does his best to keep the Corvette's power-to-weight ratio respectable, McLellan's primary mission is satisfying the current Corvette buyer hooked on comfort and convenience. Yes, this is a drastic turnabout from the Zora Arkus-Duntov era of Corvette development. Chevrolet's one and only engineering demigod did his best to keep the Corvette a half-civilized racer—not too convenient, but plenty satisfying, with a big-block prime mover stuffed under the hood. Zora made sure the right things happened when you stepped on the gas."

The right things were still happening when a driver stepped on the Corvette's gas in 1978, just not to the same degree as they had during the third-generation's early days. A lot had changed in 10 years. No-lead had turned to gold. "Internal" and "combustion" had become dirty words, although less so after all those smog controls went to work. Horsepower, too, had become taboo due to its perceived threat to innocent highway travelers. And what little was left in the high-horsepower range after 1970 had become almost impossible to insure, at least for mere mortals taking home mild-mannered paychecks.

But two things didn't change: the Corvette's basic platform and American's lust for that sexy body. "Big-blocks and Zora Arkus-Duntov have gone away together," continued Car and Driver, "leaving Dave McLellan with an 11-year-old design and at least 50,000 customers who want to buy it every year." Indeed, demand continued to overwhelm supply through the end of the decade, this even though the car essentially remained old news. Chevrolet killjoys could nail down the lid on the convertible. They could deep-six the 454. They just couldn't stop the madness, no matter how hard they tried. They kept rolling out basically the same Shark year in, year out, and fiberglass fans still kept cheering. They let power dwindle down to the nubbins and drivers still kept driving. They raised prices through the roof and buyers still kept buying.

After selling 49,213 Corvettes in 1977, Chevrolet rolled out 46,774 more in 1978, all identified with special "25th Anniversary" badging and fitted with the first major body modification to appear since 1968. McLellan's

In 1978 Chevrolet celebrated two milestones: 25 years of Corvettes and the fiberglass two-seater's first selection as Indianapolis 500 Pace Car. All 46,776 Corvettes built in 1978 wore 25th anniversary badges and 6,502 of those cars were Limited Edition Indy Pace Car replicas like the one shown here.

design team finally made its own mark on the Corvette by adding that "fastback" rear glass, "a universally appreciated Good Move," in *Car and Driver's* words. "The large rear window freshened up the Corvette's profile, and it also added space and light to help relieve the claustrophobia inside this, the most tightly coupled car known to man."

While that sloping rear window did increase storage area behind the seats, it didn't allow access to that space. Making that glass roof

a lift-up hatchback would have been the logical move. McLellan, however, opted not to complicate matters. Reaching over the Corvette's high, wide rear quarters to gain such access would not have been an easy task. At least that was the opinion around Warren. Then. Apparently Corvette customers themselves didn't give those missing hinges a second thought. They couldn't get enough of that sleek, new shell in 1978.

The production run to end all production runs then came the next year. Sales for 1979

totaled 53,807, a new all-time high that still stands today and probably will forever. Only one other model year tally has come close: the extended run for the first C4 in 1984. That year's (make that year-and-half's) final count was 51,547.

Never before had so many Corvette buyers been so willing to spend so much for so little performance. "GM's assembly plant in St. Louis cranked out more than 46,000 Corvettes last year," added *Car and Driver*, "and to the best of our knowledge, not a soul bought one for less than full sticker. The more the buyers spend, the less they seem interested in buying real sports cars. Corvette customers opt for automatic transmissions, cruise controls, and power windows in droves."

In 1969, the Corvette's long, long RPO list was dominated by dominating performance options like aluminum cylinder heads, side-mount exhausts, metallic brakes and super-duty four-speeds. By 1976 the list had

shortened considerably and among its most popular RPO codes were A31 (power windows), C60 (air conditioning), J50 (power brakes), N41 (power steering), and N37 (tilt-telescopic steering column).

The options lineup was long again in 1978, only this time it was stuffed full of the likes of the U75 power antenna, the D35 sport mirrors, the UP6 AM/FM stereo with Citizens Band radio, and the CC1 removable glass roof panels. It was all the added fluff like this that had *Road & Track*'s ever-critical critics up in arms in 1980 concerning the Corvette's latest tack, which in their minds was heading even further away from Zora's original ideal. "Someone is evidently missing the point, but is it 50,000 proud Vette buyers each year or us?"

Good question. That buyers were flocking into Chevy dealerships in record numbers to snap up a supposed performance machine that was more luxury showboat than sports car was one thing. That they continued doing so while

Exclusive seats and upholstery were included in the Indy Pace Car replica deal. Notice also the Citizens Band radio mike on the console. CB radios were Corvette options from 1978 to 1985. The AM/FM stereo with CB, RPO UP6, was amazingly popular in 1978, even at $638 a pop, good buddy. UP6 installations totaled 7,138 that year.

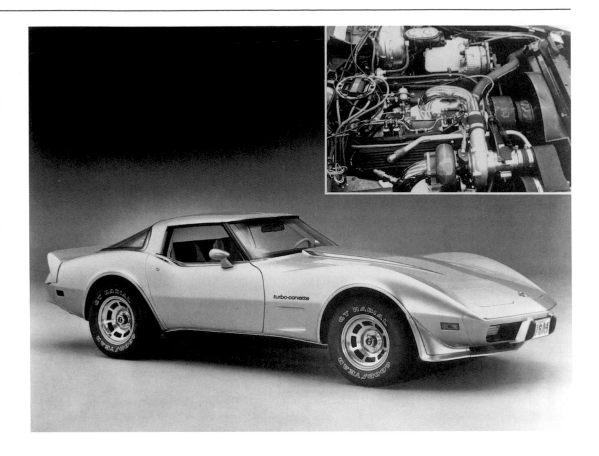

McLellan's engineers in 1979 put together this showcar to experiment with an alternative power source never tried by Duntov—turbocharging. An AIResearch TO3 turbo was combined with fuel injection to up the L-48 350's 195 horsepower to about 280 or 290, according to development engineer John Pearce. According to *Car and Driver's* Don Sherman, performance for the 1979 Turbo Corvette was only slightly better than the naturally aspirated L-82 model. Zero to 60 was 6.3 seconds for the Turbo, 6.6 clicks for the L-82. Quarter-mile time was 15-flat for the former, 15.3 for the latter. *Chevrolet Public Relations*

prices were also rising at record clips was another. It surely appeared to be a violation of the laws of economics.

A standard Corvette in 1958 cost $3,591. Ten years later the base price (for a 1968 coupe) had only risen to $4,663, an increase of 23 percent. The base sticker then skyrocketed by 100 percent over the next 10 years. A 1978 Corvette's bottom line began at $9,351.89. From there that line would shoot up by 96 percent in only five years. The 10-grand barrier was shattered in 1979 as the standard sticker reached $10,220.23. It was $13,140.24 in 1980, $16,258.52 in 1981, and a whopping $18,290.07 in 1982.

Of course not every customer was entirely willing to ride the Corvette's steep ascent up that pricing curve. Sales "dropped" to 40,614 in 1980 and 40,606 in 1981. Sure, those two figures paled a bit in comparison to 1979's lofty record. But they undoubtedly didn't disappoint Chevrolet officials, who would have been happy with anything above 25,000. As it is, 1980 and 1981's totals still stand as the sixth- and seventh-best Corvette counts ever. And those numbers looked awfully good when sales

finally did come back down to earth in 1982. "Only" 25,407 Corvettes were sold that year as buyers were distracted by rumors of an all-new fourth-generation model to come for 1983.

Helping increase the 1978–82 pricing curve's rate of climb was yet another expansion of the Corvette's standard equipment package. Once again, Chevy's decision-makers took note of customer preferences and responded accordingly. Of the 46,774 Corvettes sold in 1978, 37,858 had tilt-telescopic steering columns, 37,638 were fitted with air conditioning, and 36,931 featured power windows. All told, these three options cost $910 in 1978, $966 the following year. Then, effective May 7, 1979, this comfort/convenience trio was made a part of the standard Corvette deal, raising the base price by $706. Various other additions also eventually helped hike the 1979 standard price to $12,313.23.

As heavy as base bottom lines were during the last five years of the C3 run, most window stickers seen in 1978–82 were even heavier thanks to the droves of extra-cost equipment added on. The K30 cruise control option, introduced in 1977, was ordered 31,608 times in 1978

and was included on 96 percent of the Corvettes sold in 1982. RPO K30 cost $99 in 1978. The renamed K35 cruise control option in 1982 was priced at $165. A rear window defogger, RPO C49, appeared on 66 percent of the 1978 Corvettes built and 91 percent of the 1981s. The C49 price ranged from $95 in 1978 to $129 in 1982. Those highly coveted aluminum wheels tacked on another $340 in 1978, $458 in 1982. The installation percentage was 26 in 1978, 63 in 1979, 84 in 1980, 90 in 1981, and 66 in 1982. Easily the heaviest hit on the RPO list was the AM/FM stereo with CB radio. In 1978 it cost $638, good buddy. Five years later, Corvette drivers who wanted to always know Smokey's "20" needed to hand over $755. Only 1,987 did, compared to the 7,138 who gave a big 10-4 to the UP6 radio offering in 1978.

Performance options, meanwhile, were few and far between. The FE7 Gymkhana suspension

package was the only sport-minded chassis up-grade available from 1978 to 1982. Metallic brakes and off-road underpinnings were things of the past. New for 1978 were fatter 60-series steel-belted radials, but it took a few years for these wide white-letter treads to catch on. Pricing didn't help matters. In 1978, the P225/70R15 tire op-tion cost $51. The P225/60R15 tires, which re-quired fender trimming at the factory, wore a $216.32 tag. Two years later, the price had nearly doubled to $426.16. Optional 70-series rubber, accordingly, easily outsold those P225/60 tires each year until 1982, when the latter outnum-bered the former 3 to 1 despite a price differen-tial of $542.52 to $80.00.

Fortunately the relatively hot L-82 350 was still around as the 25th Anniversary Corvette's only optional V-8. Its output in 1978 actually increased from 210 horsepower to 220 thanks to the addition of a less restrictive exhaust system

Marvin Lloyd, then an 18-year veteran at Chevrolet's St. Louis assembly plant, performs the body drop on the last Corvette built in Missouri. The date was July 31, 1981. Corvette production had commenced at the new Bowling Green plant about two months before. *St. Louis Mercantile Library*

Corvettes at the Brickyard

Chevrolet is no stranger to The Brickyard, the fabled Indiana home to the Indianapolis 500. The Bow-Tie boys can brag of leading the pace lap at Indy more times than any other manufacturer. When a Monte Carlo did the honors on May 30, 1999, it marked the 12th occasion a Chevy product has performed as the prestigious Indy 500 pace car.

A Fleetmaster convertible was the first in 1948, followed by the sensational, all-new 1955 Bel Air seven years later. The equally sensational Camaro emerged in 1967, just in time to take its rightful place at the head of the pack at Indy that year. Camaros repeated as pace cars in 1969, 1982, and 1993. In between, a Beretta convertible toured Indy in 1990.

Curiously, Chevrolet's fiberglass two-seater was on the scene for a quarter century before it made its debut as an Indy 500 pacer in 1978. Seemingly making up for lost time, America's sports car then returned to The Brickyard for three additional encores over the next 20 years.

A convertible model rejoined the Corvette lineup after an 11-year hiatus in 1986 and was immediately chosen as the pace car for the 70th running of the greatest spectacle in motorsports. Chevrolet officials that year were more than proud of the fact that their latest Corvette needed no special engineering modifications to help bring Rick Mears, Danny Sullivan, Michael Andretti, and the rest up to speed. Save for the safety-conscious strobe lights, five-point harness and onboard fire system, the yellow, 230-horsepower ragtop that lead the pace lap on May 31, 1986, was basically identical to all the other 1986 Corvette convertibles sold to the public. The Corvette's second pace lap appearance also represented the second time that a street-legal, stone-stock machine hit the bricks at Indy. The first? Chevrolet's 1978 Corvette.

Retired U.S. Air Force Brigadier General Chuck Yeager, a man who certainly knows a little something about setting the pace, was the celebrity driver in 1986. Yeager, of course, was the first man to fly faster than the speed of sound on October 14, 1947. Flying much lower and slower, Bobby Rahal won the 1986 Indy 500.

After the race, Walter Mitty types were typically offered pace car replicas. Only this time Chevrolet considered every Corvette convertible built in 1986, 7,315 in all, to be street-going Indy pacers, regardless of color. No special adornments or limited-edition options packages were offered. It simply was left up to the buyer to add a dealer-offered commemorative decal to the doors of his or her 1986 droptop. Most didn't.

Chevrolet image-makers did things a bit differently nine years later after division general manager Jim Perkins drove the third Corvette to pace the Indy 500 around the legendary track on May 28, 1995. This time a truly limited limited-edition pace car replica package was offered. Not even a blind man could miss this one. Only 527 Indy 500 Pace Car Replica convertibles were sold, all wearing a Dark Purple and Arctic White finish with perhaps the splashiest graphics yet seen on a commemorative pacer. Completing the deal, listed as RPO Z4Z, were special leather seats embroidered with Indianapolis 500 logos. Price for the Z4Z option was an eye-popping $2,816.

Even more eye-popping, in terms of both visual impact and the bottom line, was the fourth Indy pace car Corvette, this one based on the totally redesigned C5 platform. When introduced in 1997, the C5 came only in targa-top form. Convertible lovers had to wait a year. By the time a topless C5 did appear in 1998 it was already a foregone conclusion that this sexy, speedy soft-top would be chosen to set the pace at Indianapolis.

Once again the Corvette needed no additional wrench-turning to do the job. With the 345-horse LS1 up front, the 1998 C5 easily ranked as the most capable Indy pace car Corvette yet. And if you thought the 1995 pace car stood out in a crowd . . .

The second-edition Z4Z Indy Pace Car Replica package included even higher doses of high-profile imagery. Glowing Radar Blue paint was accented by glaring yellow graphics that ran down each side and culminated in a checkered flag flowing up over the rear wheels onto the rear deck. Screaming yellow wheels, yellow stripes on the hood, and yellow inserts for the black leather seats added further exclamation.

Additional Z4Z equipment included electronic dual-zone heating and air conditioning, a Delco AM/FM radio/CD player with Bose speakers, memory package, Theft Lock, a digital clock, and floor mats. The JL4 Active Handling system, a new option priced at $500 for 1998 C5s, was also included in the Z4Z options group. The 4L60-E four-speed automatic transmission was "standard" at no extra cost. Adding the six-speed manual required another $815 on top of the $5,039 Z4Z asking price. Total production for the wallet-wilting 1998 Indy Pace Car Replica was 1,163.

The Corvette will, without a doubt, be back on track at Indianapolis soon enough—as part of the 50th anniversary celebration in 2003 perhaps?

The Corvette's first appearance as the prestigious pace car for the Indianapolis 500 came in 1978. A street-going pace car replica (on left) of course followed. Corvettes have since paced Indy three more times, with replicas also being produced in 1986 (top), 1995 (right), and 1998. *Chevrolet Public Relations*

The first Corvette rolled off the Bowling Green assembly line in Kentucky on June 1, 1981. Eleven years later, the 1 millionth Corvette (shown here) was built there on July 2, 1992. *Chevrolet Public Relations*

and a dual-snorkel air induction setup that improved breathing on the top end. Engineers were just then figuring out how to reverse the downward performance spiral created by ever-tightening emissions standards and demands for better fuel economy. Results of this roller-coaster ride up a new learning curve even included a power boost for the standard L-48 350, which went from 180 horsepower in 1977 to

185 in 1978. L-48s sold in California and high altitudes that year were rated at 175 horses.

Either way, L-48 or L-82, the quarter-century-old Corvette remained this country's top performance automobile. Or so said *Car and Driver* in a turnabout of opinion late in 1977. "After a number of recent Corvette editions that prompted us to mourn the steady decline of both performance and quality in this

Chevrolet stopped offering Tuxedo Black paint as a Corvette option in 1969. Black returned in 1977. Some black Corvettes were sold in 1975 and 1976, but not necessarily by Chevrolet. A special paint option in those years allowed buyers to take delivery of their car in primer. They could then have it painted in any color they preferred. This L-82 Corvette is one of 10,465 ordered through regular channels in black in 1979. Black was by far the most popular Corvette color that year, outnumbering the second-favorite, white, by nearly 2,000 sprayings.

once-proud marque, we can happily report the 25th example of the Corvette is much improved across the board. Not only will it run faster now—the L-82 version with four-speed is certainly the fastest American production car, while the base L-48 automatic is no slouch—but the general drivability and road manners are of a high order as well." L-48 performance was quoted at 7.8 seconds for the time-honored 0-60 run, 123 miles per hour on the top end. The L-82 reportedly could reach 133 miles per hour.

Additional tweaking increased L-82 output to 225 horsepower in 1979. The L-48 that year also received the L-82's dual-snorkel induction equipment and "open flow" mufflers, which helped up its output ante to 195 horsepower. Although the L-82 350 received another power boost to 230 horses in 1980, it was the end of the line for the Corvette's last optional "hi-perf" V-8. Engineers were never able to certify the "high-compression" (9:1) L-82 for sale in California during the years 1978 to 1980. Chevrolet then cancelled the L-82 option outright, leaving a 190-horsepower 350 as the only power choice in 1981.

Corvette buyers in California were limited to one engine only, the base 350, since 1976. Then that state's extra-strict emissions standards were tightened even further in 1980.

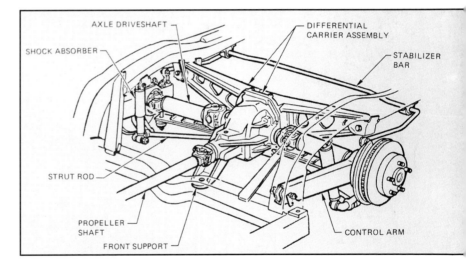

Dave McLellan's main goal during the C3 years was to shave off as many pounds as possible from the platform to try to improve performance through the back door. Various lightened components—including aluminum wheels, tubular steel headers (instead of cast-iron exhaust manifolds), and magnesium valve covers—were introduced during his tenure. In 1980 a new differential housing and corresponding frame cross-member, both done in aluminum, were installed.

Chevrolet began offering contrasting paint schemes for the Corvette in 1956. The "440" code exterior finish added a second color to the bodyside "cove" panels. This option was dropped after 1961. Two-tone paint schemes returned in 1978 for the Indy Pace Car replica and Silver Anniversary models. Then came RPO D84 in 1981. All D84 two-tone Corvettes that year were created in Bowling Green to help show off the new assembly plant's superior paint facilities. This beige/dark bronze Corvette is one of 5,352 two-tone cars sold in 1981. Another 4,871 D84 cars were finished out in 1982.

Chevrolet failed to certify either of its 350-ci V-8s for sale there that year. So in place of the 190-horsepower L-48 (and in exchange for a $50 credit) came the LG4 305-ci V-8. Although it was taken right from the mundane passenger-car parts shelf, the West Coast-legal LG4 still produced only 10 fewer horses than the L-48 thanks to the use of stainless-steel tubular headers and a "Computer Command Control" system that automatically adjusted carburetor mixture and ignition timing on demand. LG4 sales in 1980 totaled 3,221.

The LG4's lightweight headers (with oxygen-sensor smog controls) and computer "brain box" were transferred to a new 350 small-block, the L-81, in 1981. Not only was this 190-horsepower V-8 certified for sale in all 50 states, it was also available in California with either a four-speed or an automatic transmission. This meant a bushy, bushy blonde beach boy could specify a bitchin' manual-trans Corvette for the first time since 1975. But he could only do so for one brief year. Chevrolet didn't offer a four-speed stick at all for the 1982 Corvette in any state. Not since 1954 had a complete model-year run been limited only to automatic transmission installations. Luckily a four-speed option returned for the new C4 Corvette in 1984.

Various other features on the new next-generation Corvette were also "returning." McLellan's engineers had been working on the C4 since 1978, and more than once over the following years they let some of that developing technology slip out into the latest C3 model. Easily the biggest slip came in 1982 when an intriguing new powerplant appeared for the final third-generation Corvette.

"It's a harbinger of things to come," said McLellan about that car that preceded his sport coupe de grace. "For the 1982 model is more than just the last of a generation; it's stage one of a two-stage production. We're doing the power team this year. Next year, we add complete new styling and other innovations."

While Corvette fans would have to wait more than half a year to finally see the redesigned C4 in the spring of 1983, they got to try out the new car's engine and transmission some 18 months before. Designated L-83, the 1982 Corvette's 350 V-8 used refined versions of the tubular-header exhaust system and Computer Command Control equipment that

first appeared along with the LG4 California V-8 in 1980. And like the L-81 350 of 1981, the L-83 also used weight-saving magnesium valve covers. The real news, however, came atop the engine.

McLellan's men called it "Cross Fire Injection." To many witnesses, the setup looked very much like the rare, twin-carb option used on some Z/28 Camaros in 1969. But those weren't carburetors beneath that cool-looking air cleaner. They were two computer-controlled Rochester throttle-body fuel-injection units mounted diagonally on an aluminum cross-ram intake manifold. Making this TBI (throttle body injection) system work was an ECM—Electronic Control Module—that was capable of dealing with up to 80 variables (ignition

A federal law required all 1980 automobiles, including America's only sports car, to be fitted with speedometers reading no higher than 85 miles per hour. Performance by then was down, but not that low. Shown here is the emasculated speedo in an 1981 Corvette.

The third-generation Corvette run ended with an exclamation point in the form of the 1982 Collectors Edition. Special paint and wheels were part of the package, as were extra-wide white-letter tires. Replacement rubber has long since replaced those P225/60R-15 treads on this Collectors Edition Corvette.

Exclusive leather upholstery, luxury carpeting, multitoned door panel treatment, and a leather-wrapped steering wheel were standard inside the 1982 Collectors Edition. A new four-speed automatic transmission with a lock-up torque converter and automatic overdrive was also standard. Chevrolet didn't bother certifying a four-speed in 1982, making this the first time since late in 1955 (a few three-speed manuals were installed near the end of the 1955 run) that all Corvettes built in a given year were automatics.

timing, fuel/air mixture, idle speed, and so on) adjustments per second to maximize performance and efficiency. Although this TBI setup wasn't exactly a fuel-injection system in the truest sense of the term—not like the Rochester-supplied unit used by Corvettes from 1957 to 1965—it did produce something former fuelie drivers were familiar with: instant throttle response.

Enhancing overall response even further was the new 700-R4 four-speed automatic transmission, which was also electronically linked to the ECM. Shifts and the torque converter's lockup clutch feature were all precisely controlled by the ECM depending on varying speed and load data inputs. This power team combo clearly was as high as high tech had ever been beneath a fiberglass hood to that point. Yet even with all that techno-wizardy, the 1982 small-block still only produced 200 horsepower. "A far cry from the 400 bhp-plus days of the L88 and L68," began Road & Track's verdict on the last C3, "but not exactly a shrinking violet by today's wheezing standards."

McLellan's plans to put those 200 humble horses to work most effectively involved putting the Corvette on a diet. Accordingly, the new C4 in 1984 was lousy with weight-saving

aluminum components, including a lightweight differential housing and corresponding frame mount first introduced in 1980. The 1984 Corvette also relied on a fiberglass mono-leaf spring in place of the steel multileaf unit used by most third-generation Corvettes. This idea first appeared in 1981 for automatic cars with standard suspensions. The plastic mono-leaf weighed only 8 pounds. The steel leaf spring setup it replaced tipped the scales at 44 pounds.

To both showcase all this new technology and mark the end of the Shark era, Chevrolet in 1982 put together a special model the likes of which Corvette buyers had never seen before. The 1982 Collector Edition was, in Dave McLellan's words, "a unique combination of color, equipment, and innovation [resulting in] one of the most comprehensive packages ever offered to the Corvette buyer." Actually Corvette customers had cast their eyes on something similar just five years before as the 1978–82 group featured special-edition offerings at its bookends. The Collector Edition helped close things out in 1982. Kicking off the fastback years in 1978 was the Limited Edition Corvette.

Casual witnesses and disappointed investors alike best remember that 1978 model as

Removable glass roof panels topped off the Collectors Edition, while a welcomed hatchback window brought up the rear. The optional power antenna was also included in the $22,537 deal.

Many thought the 1982 Corvette's 200-horsepower 350 small-block was fitted with dual four-barrel carburetors. But beneath that air cleaner were twin throttle-body injectors. Used by both the Corvette and Camaro, this TBI setup was called "Cross-Fire Injection", even though it wasn't fuel injection in the true sense of the term. Tuned-port injection (TPI) design debuted in 1985, and this actually represented the "fuelie" Corvette's return after a 20-year hiatus. *Chevrolet Motor Division*

the Indy Pace Car replica. For the first time, America's only sports car was chosen that year as the Indianapolis 500's prestigious pacer. And just as they had done with Camaro Indy pacers in 1967 and 1969, Chevrolet officials opted to put special pace car replicas on the street in 1978 to help mark the moment.

As the name implied, the original plan was to make this package a limited-edition collector's piece. The *Wall Street Journal* even went so far as to print a cover story in March 1978 touting the Indy Pace Car Corvette as a sure-fire ride to riches. Those lucky enough to get their hands on one of these rare machines reportedly would be able to turn it around for many times its original sales price after only a matter of months. Initially the window sticker read $13,653.21, $4,300 more than a base 25th anniversary Corvette coupe. Once word got around, however, the going price soared as high as $30,000. Those unlucky enough to buy at that price soon found out that some old adages never lie: If it sounds to good to be true, it probably is.

Perhaps that adage would not have rang so honestly had Chevrolet only built 300 Indy

Pace Car Corvettes as originally planned. But all speculation ran right down the drain after Chevy's litigation-shy decisionmakers decided to build at least one Pace Car replica for every dealer in America. Apparently the idea was to avoid any lawsuits from potential buyers or dealers (translated: opportunistic exploiters) left in the lurch with nothing save for complaints of unfair, monopolistic sales practices. Whatever the case, the final "limited-edition" count for the 1978 Indy Pace Car's production run reached 6,502. Most (if not all) of those who originally jumped on the Limited Edition Corvette bandwagon 20 years ago are still waiting to make hay today.

Included in the Limited Edition's original price, however astronomical, was a long list of options combined with a heavy dose of special treatments. On the outside was an exclusive black-over-silver two-tone paint scheme accented by red pinstriping. Official Indy 500 decals were expected. A front air dam, rear spoiler, aluminum wheels (also with red pinstripes), and glass T-tops were part of the deal as well. Inside was an exclusive leather interior

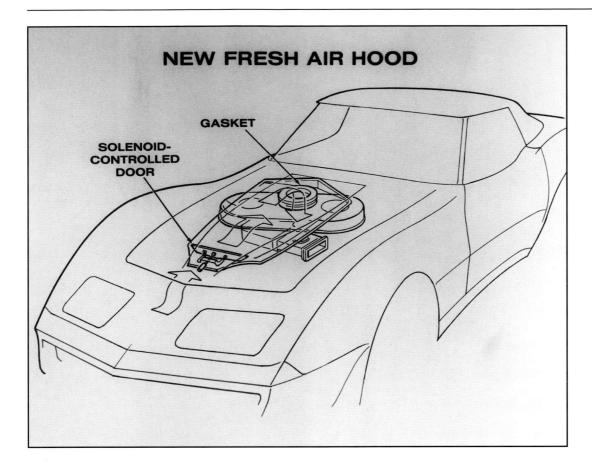

NEW FRESH AIR HOOD

SOLENOID-
CONTROLLED
DOOR

GASKET

The 1982 Corvette was also fitted with a new air-induction hood that directed some of the radiator's cooling flows into a special duct formed into the hood's underside. At the front of the duct was a solenoid-controlled flap that opened on demand. Cooler, denser air then rushed to the duct's rear where it flowed through an opening in the air cleaner's top, which was sealed to the hood. *Chevrolet Motor Division*

done in silver-gray—called "smoke" by Chevrolet. Lightweight buckets were also exclusive to the Limited Edition's interior. Optional extras included in the Indy Pace Car package were power windows, door locks and antenna; a rear window defogger; air conditioning; sport mirrors; tilt-telescopic steering column; white-letter P225/60R15 tires; heavy-duty battery; AM/FM 8-track stereo with dual rear speakers; and the Convenience Group. Included in that last collection, RPO ZX2, were a dome light delay, headlight warning buzzer, underhood light, low-fuel warning light, interior courtesy light, floor mats, intermittent wipers, and passenger-side vanity mirror on the visor.

For those who wanted to bridge the gap between the standard 1978 Corvette with its 25th anniversary badges and the heavily loaded, high-priced Indy Pace Car replica, there was the Silver Anniversary option, RPO B2Z. Priced at $399, the B2Z package added another exclusive two-tone paint scheme, this one done in light silver over dark silver. Dual sport mirrors and aluminum wheels were required options along with that commemorative paint.

Silver Anniversary Corvette production in 1978 was 15,283.

Optional two-tone paint would return to the Corvette's RPO list in 1981, again wearing a $399 price tag. Four D84 combinations—Silver/Dark Blue, Silver/Charcoal, Beige/Dark Bronze, and Autumn Red/Dark Claret—were offered, with sales of those combinations totaling 5,352. The D84 price rose to $428 in 1982 and included three new combos—White/Silver, Silver/Dark Claret, and Silver Blue/Dark Blue—along with 1981's Silver/Charcoal. Total two-tone paint sales in 1982 hit 4,871.

Like the Silver Anniversary Corvette, the Indy Pace Car of 1978 also didn't just roll off into the sunset without passing something on to later models. The Limited Edition Corvette's high-back bucket seats became standard equipment in 1979. But not everyone thought this was an improvement. *Car and Driver* called the far-from-form-fitting bucket "an abysmal failure." "The new seats were sold to management on their weight-savings merit, and their molded-plastic design is in fact 22 pounds lighter," continued the *C/D* complaint.

It's doubtful any future Corvette generation will break the longevity record of the C3. Fifteen years is a long time, especially in today's automotive market where the "what have you done for me lately" attitude prevails like never before.

The fourth generation came close, although not by plan. Talk of an all-new, totally redesigned fifth-generation Corvette began as early as 1988. The hope then was to introduce it in time for the car's 40th anniversary in 1993. That would have cut the C4 run off at 9 years, leaving the 10-year history of the original solid-axle Corvette as the second longest span among the five generations. But C5 development was delayed again and again as GM went awash in red ink. In its place, the C4 continued rolling on for 13 years before the book was finally closed at the end of 1996.

How soon they forget. In the mad rush to laud the C5 as the best Vette yet, few onlookers in early 1997 seemed to recall a similar sensation seen nearly a decade and a half before. Like the C5, the first C4 was honored by *Motor Trend* as its prestigious "Car of the Year," and rightly so. Okay, the C5's award didn't come until the convertible version was introduced in 1998, but that's only because the targa-topped sport coupe initially unveiled in January 1997 appeared too late to make *Motor Trend's* 1997 balloting.

Dave McLellan's claim to fame as Corvette chief engineer came in March 1983 when the redesigned 1984 Corvette was introduced. Shown here is serial number 00001, the "first 1984 Corvette." This car originally was raffled away as part of a charity promotion.

The first C4 showed up tardy for its coming-out party too. Dealer introductions for the Shark's long-awaited replacement didn't begin until March 1983. By then Chevrolet officials had already decided to simply forego an official 1983 model year entirely. The last C3 was the 1982 model. The first C4 was the 1984. No 1983 Corvettes were sold to the public.

Chevrolet's extended 1984 run for its newest two-seat sensation then resulted in a near-record production total. The 51,547 1984 Corvettes built stands second only to the 53,807 produced for 1979. Forget Joe Dimaggio's 56-game hit streak; that 1979 Corvette standard without a doubt will stand forever. Will the market ever again bear such excess? Will demand ever again inspire such a supply? Will Chevrolet ever again sell 50,000 Corvettes in a year? Ask these questions again in 2003.

Such sales success like that of 1979 represented one of the main reasons why the C3 was allowed to run for so long. C4 roots originally took hold in 1978 with the plan then being to introduce the car as a 1982 model. Yet, despite a national recession, the Corvette entered the 1980s selling stronger than ever. Yearly production for both 1980 and 1981 surpassed 40,000. Why fix something that wasn't broken?

On top of that, Chevrolet officials also didn't want to tackle start-up tasks for both a new assembly line and a new model at the same time. Corvette production at the Bowling Green facility began in June 1981 with the venerable C3 remaining the focus. Various development gremlins then surfaced, like they do so often, to help delay the C4's introduction further. Most agreed, however, that the end result was worth the wait.

In their February 1984 Car of the Year issue, *Motor Trend's* editors concluded that the C4 had risen to a new plateau. "The [1984] Corvette has the highest EQ [Excitement Quotient] of anything to come out of an American factory. Ever. Its handling goes beyond mere competence; call it superb, call it leading edge, call it World Class. *We* certainly do."

Indeed it was the C4's new chassis that set it apart from what came before. Highlights included transverse, mono-leaf fiberglass springs front and rear; Girling four-wheel disc brakes; revised suspension locations at both ends; and the liberal use of aluminum components throughout to save weight. Independent suspension continued in back, but it was improved markedly with a five-link design in place of the old three-link setup. On the clean side of the car, a totally fresh restyle incorporated improved function into its form by way of a large "clamshell" hood that allowed easier engine access.

Later C4 upgrades included the introduction of the fuel-injected L98 in 1985, a convertible Corvette's return in 1986, the ZR-1's emergence in 1990, the rise of the LT1 in 1992, and the LT4 and Grand Sport debuts in 1996. Fans of the fourth-generation Corvette certainly have a lot to remember.

That so much history was overshadowed with seemingly no regrets in 1997 simply helped demonstrate the C5's own historic nature. This truly was the first all-new Corvette. All other next-generation models before brought along something from their past—the first C4 still relied on the C3's Cross-Fire 350 V-8 used in 1982. Hell, even the original Corvette in 1953 borrowed many of its components from Chevrolet's mundane passenger-car parts bins. Everything about the C5 was engineered exclusively to help make this the best Corvette yet. Chief Engineer David Hill's goal was to create the most comfortable, most convenient, easiest to handle, hardest charging Corvette of all time. He didn't disappoint.

Listing the C5's impressive roll call is not something easily done in a few hundred words. Or a few thousand. The incredibly durable, wonderfully efficient, wildly powerful LS1 V-8 could fill a book all on its own. Then there's the world-class chassis with its rear-mounted transmission for better balance, the incredibly rigid frame with its central tunnel and hydro-formed side rails, and that beautiful body that cuts through the wind like no other Corvette shape before.

So much of what makes the C5 the best generation yet involves that new frame. Its super strength means that nearly all of the creaks, rattles, and rolls inherent to the C4 design are gone. Its rigidity allowed engineers to dial in much more precise suspension settings—with next to no frame flex, suspension location geometry basically remains constant and true. All this adds up to a more sure-footed, more comfortable ride. The C5 not only handles at extremes better than any previous

Corvette, it also leaves passengers with more positive seat-of-the-pants impressions in everyday driving. And dress-wearing drivers will appreciate the lower doorsills—made possible by those hydroformed frame rails—that make getting in and out less of a reach for the feet.

All this sure-footed comfort is especially apparent to convertible drivers. Even though the droptop model was introduced later in 1998, the C5 platform was essentially designed first as a convertible. Unlike a C4 convertible, which required extra bracing to compensate for its missing roof, the C5 convertible needs no major additions to keep itself in shape. This also means no extra unwanted weight is added into the convertible equation, an inherent physical law common to ragtop construction since the beginning of time.

C5 convertible owners can also take their car to the club with little muss or fuss thanks to that trunk in back, a Corvette feature last seen in 1962. Chevrolet promotional people in 1998 were more than willing to point out that the new Corvette trunk was capable of carrying not one, but two golf bags. In 1999, a third C5 variation—the lighter, lesser-priced fixed-roof coupe, or hardtop as Chevy calls it—was also fitted with a trunk. This introduction meant that, for the first time ever, Corvette buyers were faced with three different models to choose from.

More than 30,000 customers chose the C5 in 1998. Continued sales success in such quantities will certainly guarantee a long, happy life for the fifth-generation Corvette. But the C5 still has a long way to go to reach the C3's record. Indeed, 15 years is a long time.

A convertible Corvette was again reborn one year after the sensational C5 debuted in 1997. Droptop C5s were not built that first year. They appeared in 1998 just in time for *Motor Trend* to name the latest, greatest Corvette its "Car of the Year."

Everything beneath the 1982 Corvette's skin worked in unison to maximize both performance and efficiency. Chevy promotional people also bragged of the car's new low-restriction "dual exhaust system"—it was, of course, still the same design used beneath Corvettes since 1975. Exhaust flow, however, was improved by a freer-flowing catalytic converter. Also improved was the Cross-Fire Injection V-8's new computer, which could adjust fuel flow as much as 80 times a second. The 1981 computer-controlled carburetor's best variable adjustment rate was 10 times per second.

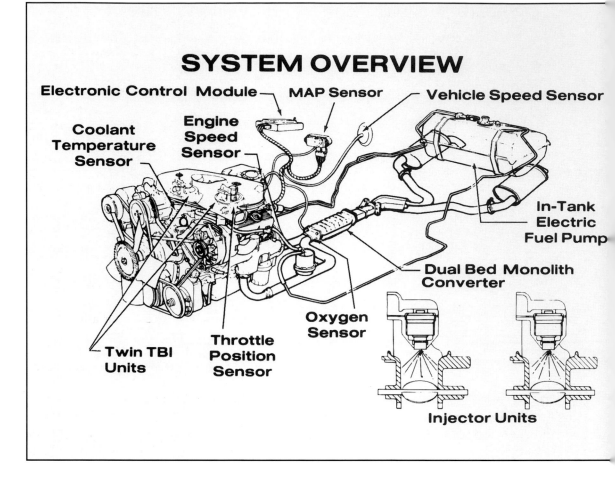

SYSTEM OVERVIEW

"The problem with parts engineered down to the last ounce is that aesthetic appeal is often-times the first pound to go. The Corvette's seat shells have the throwaway feel of parts molded by Rubbermaid."

While critics could be picky about their seats, they couldn't complain about another Indy Pace Car feature carried over into 1979. Those front and rear spoilers added on in 1978 became an option, RPO D80, the following year. Priced at $265, the D80 spoilers found their way onto 6,853 Corvettes in 1979 and went a long way toward reducing unwanted drag. In 1980, new front and rear caps with integral spoilers were added.

Yet another exterior modification appeared two years later. Available only for the Collector Edition, frameless hatchback glass was hinged on in 1982 to technically expand Corvette bodystyle choices to two for the first time since the convertible departed after 1975. Apparently McLellan and crew decided that anyone able to pay the extra asking price for

the 1982 Collector Edition probably would have some hired help on hand to do all that long-reach loading into and out of the rear storage area.

At 18 grand, a base Corvette in 1982 was already expensive enough. Fully loaded with options and extras like the 1978 Indy Pace Car, the Collector Edition became the first Corvette to enter the $20,000 zone. The exact suggested price was $22,537.59, $4,250 more than that standard sport coupe. Helping hike that price up were exclusive "turbine" alloy wheels wearing white-letter P255/60R15 Goodyear Eagle GT rubber, glass roof panels done in unique bronze tinting, a rear window defogger, a power antenna, and special identification inside and out.

Like the Limited Edition and Silver Anniversary Corvettes of 1978, the 1982 Collector Edition featured unique paint, this time a silver-beige finish accented by graduated gray decals and accent striping. That exclusive color carried over inside, where silver-beige leather was found on the seats and door panels. Leather wrapping also went onto the steering wheel and luxurious, extra-deep pile carpeting covered the floor.

Unlike the 1978 Limited Edition model, the 1982 Collector Edition did not tease potential collectors into a frenzy. "The Collector Edition is sure to become a hot item, much like the Indy Pace Car in 1978," wrote *Road & Track*'s Joe Rusz. "You may recall that because of their scarcity, Pace Cars sold for as much as $28,000, about double the sticker price. McLellan tells me this won't happen with the Collector Edition because the new Bowling Green plant will turn out as many cars as the market will bear." Indeed, the new Kentucky home to the Corvette built Collector Edition models as fast as demand demanded. It was that simple: no leading on, no lawsuits. When the demand finally stopped, the final count for the year was 6,759.

While the Collector Edition did honor the Corvette's third-generation on its way into the history books, it also helped mark the opening of a new age, the Bowling Green era, if you will. Chevrolet officials wanted to show off the new Kentucky plant's advanced paint facility, and the attractive Collector Edition proved to be just the ticket to do just that.

Actually it was those two-tone Corvettes that debuted in 1981 that first demonstrated the new assembly facility's merits. The book finally closed on the St. Louis story on August 1, 1981, as the finishing touches were put on the last Missouri-built Corvette. The first Kentucky-built model had rolled off the new Bowling Green line on June 1, meaning the Corvette's past briefly overlapped its future. Solid-colored Corvettes built in St. Louis that year were done in lacquer as always. Meanwhile, Bowling Green rolled out two-tone after two-tone using a new enamel-based paint enhanced with clearcoats. Of the 40,606 Corvettes built for 1981, 8,955 began life in Kentucky.

Rumors of a move to a larger, more modern plant began surfacing along the Mississippi as early as 1973. Built in 1920, the Chevrolet plant in St. Louis was not only archaic, it was also severely limited in size and scope. That the Corvette team had managed to build nearly 50,000 cars a year there during those hot-to-trot years in the late 1970s was more a

testament to their dedication than it was proof that the Fisher Mill Building, located on Natural Bridge Avenue, was capable of carrying on into the 1980s.

Corvette production had moved into the Fisher Mill Building just before Christmas 1953. "We selected St. Louis as the exclusive source of Corvette manufacture because the city has a central location and excellent shipping facilities and we have always found here an ample supply of competent labor," explained Edward Kelly, Chevrolet Motor Division's general manufacturing manager. The first Corvettes began forming in St. Louis on December 28, 1953. Some 25 years and three generations later it had become painfully obvious that the legacy had run as far it could. Environmental Protection Agency cops were hounding officials at the aging plant about its paint facility, which wasn't anywhere near up to snuff as far as federal air quality standards were concerned. And Dave McLellan knew full well that his baby, the planned C4, could never be born in St. Louis. Cutting-edge innovation and obsolete production facilities just didn't mix.

The solution to the problem was a 550,000-square-foot complex formerly used by the Air Temp Division of Chrysler Corporation and the Fedders Corporation in Bowling Green. GM bought this building, expanded it to 1 million square feet and modernized it with the latest in state-of-the-art assembly technology. Most important, this new assembly plant wouldn't be home to anything but fiberglass two-seaters. "The Bowling Green facility, which will build Corvettes exclusively, is an investment in Corvette's future," explained a 1981 Corvette brochure. "It represents the experience and knowledge learned over all those years [in St. Louis]."

So it was that a new, thoroughly modern production facility was up and running in time to build a new, thoroughly exciting fiberglass two-seater for 1984. After 15 years, the Shark's tale finally came to a close in 1982. As for the old St. Louis plant, it was boarded up in the fall of 1987 after building 13 million Chevrolet cars and trucks. About a half million of those were third-generation renditions of America's only sports car. Call them rough, call them soft, it didn't matter. They were all Corvettes.

Enough said.

Index